SPIRALING UPWARD

HOPE AND HEALING AFTER

ADDICTION, MANIA, AND EVEN CANCER

Jason Hollen

Copyright © 2020 by Jason Hollen

All rights reserved.

www.spiralingministries.org

ISBN: 978-1-7331023-6-0

Published by Fitting Words LLC. www.fittingwords.net

No part of this book may be reproduced in any form or by any electronic or mechanical means including information storage and retrieval systems, without permission in writing from the author. The only exception is by a reviewer, who may quote short excerpts in a review.

The author has tried to recreate events, locales, and conversations from his memories of them. In order to maintain their anonymity in some instances, the author has changed the names of individuals and places. This book is not intended as a substitute for the medical advice of physicians. The reader should regularly consult a physician in matters relating to his/her health and particularly with respect to any symptoms that may require diagnosis or medical attention.

Scripture quotations are from The ESV® Bible (The Holy Bible, English Standard Version®), copyright © 2001 by Crossway, a publishing ministry of Good News Publishers. Used by permission. All rights reserved.

Cover design by LA Creative. www.lacreative09.com

Dedicated to my amazing wife, Kristyn. You stood by me when I was in the depths of Hell. Throughout my addiction—and nursing me back to health after my battle with cancer—you never gave up on me, and would not let me give up on myself. I am forever grateful for your love and support. I star you.

"I can do all things through Christ who strengthens me."
—Philippians 4:13

Table of Contents

Foreword	11
Chapter 1: Seriously?	13
Chapter 2: The Battles Begin	17
Chapter 3: The Downward Spiral	33
Chapter 4: Locked Away	50
Chapter 5: I Star You	66
Chapter 6: Preparing to Launch	77
Chapter 7: A Final Trip Down	91
Chapter 8: True Restoration	103
Chapter 9: The Dreaded "C" Word	119
Chapter 10: Funny Little Cigarettes	140
Chapter 11: Spiraling Ministries	152
Chapter 12: Clean & Sober...and Thriving	164
Appendix I: About Spiraling Ministries	179
Appendix II: Spiraling Ministries Statement of Faith	180
Appendix III: Suggested Resources	186

FOREWORD

by Michael Perron

Candor and honesty—traits you'll get from Jason Hollen through his book *Spiraling Upward*. It's difficult, if not impossible, for any of us to find true recovery without an assessment of our current state. The world tells us to look for excuses, but Hollen looked within and knew he couldn't tell his story without telling his whole story, even if it was sometimes painful.

As a recovered addict, I know the demon that attempts to convince you of its lofty opinion.

The voice that tells you, "You're hopeless," "Why don't you just give up?" "Just end it all right now—the world would be a better place if you did."

That opinion is a lie, one that is in direct contradiction to the knowledge of God.

Jason certainly heard that voice from a young age. Thankfully, he eventually shut it out and has now published a work that will help you break free from the lies of the Enemy and listen to the voice of truth. That is, if you're willing to listen. No one suggests it's easy, but it's absolutely possible.

As the pastor of Life Recovery at Prestonwood Baptist Church, I've witnessed many lives transformed through the love of Jesus Christ. Isaiah 41:10 rings true: "So do not fear, for I am with you; do not be dismayed, for I am your God. I will strengthen you and help you; I will uphold you with my righteous right hand." I believe Hollen's book reveals that and is a needed resource for those struggling and those with loved ones seeking support.

The captivity brought on by crippling addiction, abuse, and a fight with cancer is no joke. Jason's openness about those struggles reveals the miraculous work God did in his life. His life was a mess, and in the pages that follow is the story of how your "mess" can be your "message" to someone else.

Enjoy the read and consider who else might be blessed by it.

Chapter 1:
Seriously?

Fasten your seatbelt. You're not going to believe what I'm about to tell you. But, I assure you, it really did happen. When I tell stories from my life, I see the look in people's eyes. The "you're full of it" look. I don't blame them. You see, I'm an addict. I've put more things into my body than I can count. That's not all. Outside forces have also wrecked both my mind and body. Those forces have attacked me with a vengeance, and with brutal honesty, I'll share how I've attacked myself, my family, and friends. Parts are ugly. I mean hideous. But, there's also a beautiful story of redemption. I'm still standing, and I want to take you on that journey.

Seriously? It's a legitimate question. It's the same one I've asked myself often the morning after a drug or booze-filled evening. That is, if I could even remember what happened the night before. I mean, seriously? Why would I do the same stupid thing one night after another? Why would I compound the problem by drinking margaritas at lunch on a workday and then snorting a line of cocaine in the afternoon? Who does that? Well, I do. At least, I did. It's only by God's grace I can now say "did." Past tense. I thank the Lord for saving me. Physically. Mentally. Spiritually.

I had a lot of crap going on starting from an early age. Think of a particular addiction and what age a person would normally begin abusing that substance. Then subtract five years from the age. That's me. I broke all the norms. You'll read all of that in the coming pages. Let me ask you a favor. A plea, really. Stick with me through this life journey.

There are parts where you may say, "I can't stand the way little Jason was treated."

Fast forward a couple of chapters.

Eye roll. "I want to smack this kid, Jason. What was he thinking?"

Trust me. You'll say it.

Well, I wasn't thinking. Not in any normal sense. Not in the right mind. I had a disease. Let me issue you my first disclaimer here, and there are plenty more where this one comes from. I'm not blaming all my actions on this person or that person, a poorly dealt hand, karma, a voodoo doll, or godsmacking (I'll explain that one later). I was absolutely a co-conspirator, if not an instigator, in many of my mischievous actions. My relationship with bad actions is...well...it's complicated.

It's sort of like a fork in the road.

One is a road of love, sunshine, happy thoughts, all that stuff. The other road has potholes, darkness, impending doom. I absolutely wished I'd have steered onto that sweet road of love. However, someone else had the wheel. It happens to lots of people. Someone points them in a negative direction. The dark road. Sometimes they manage to avoid the potholes. They're mere speedbumps in life. Not me. I hit every single pothole. Sometimes, I backed up and hit the same ones again. It's sort of like punching oneself in the face.

To continue the analogy, imagine there's a cliff at the end. I raced for it with reckless abandon. The good news…no…the great news is that once a person heads down that dark road, there's a way off. An exit toward the good road. It's not a perfect road, but so much better than the dark one. Just like there are those that steered me onto the dark road, God placed people in my life that redirected my path. Lots of great friends. Most importantly, one person, a friend, who I now call my soulmate.

I met my bride, Kristyn, in high school. A thousand times she should have given up on me. No one would have blamed her. However, God gave her a tenacity unlike any other. That's a weird adjective to describe a wife. I can think of many other such adjectives, and I will add them ad nauseam throughout, but for now, I want you to know how her grit and determination lie at the core of the man I am today. I'm not saying she trumps God. He is my creator and savior, but He has used her as the main instrument in my recovery—mentally, physically, and spiritually.

I'm sure that when we both heard that I had cancer, she thought, "Seriously? Now, this?"

I had the fight of my life on my hands. But we both fought. I don't mean that she stood in my corner between rounds as the enemy punched me. I mean she stood tall in the ring with me. "I'm your

Huckleberry" from the film *Tombstone*, describes her exactly. God made her the right person for the right job at the right time.

This is my story, but it's also our story, and she'll offer her insights into doing life with me at the end of most chapters. This will take you inside our household and how she loved me when I was unlovable.

I want the addict to read this and know that a lifetime of hope and healing are available. I also want the spouse, parent, child, or friend that loves the addict to know that hope and healing are available for them as well. The overwhelming strain from addiction tests the strongest of relationships. I want all parties to know that hope exists. I found it. I now embrace it.

I'm struck by a passage in the seventh chapter of Romans written by the apostle Paul. "For I do not understand my own actions. For I do not do what I want, but I do the very thing I hate." That's verse fifteen.

Now eighteen. "For I know that nothing good dwells in me, that is, in my flesh. For I have the desire to do what is right, but not the ability to carry it out." Ouch! Sometimes reading the Bible hits you hard. The truth hurts. That violent war raged within me with tons of collateral damage as I spiraled out of control.

Remember in the television show *Lost* where they had flashbacks, flash forwards, and this thing called flash sideways? Well, I didn't just spiral down, I spiraled sideways, forward, backward, but mostly down. The dictionary defines a downward spiral as a series of decisions, actions, or events that make a situation progressively worse. An upward spiral would seemingly be the opposite, right? It would constitute decisions, actions, and events that make a situation progressively better. That's the story I want for you. A story of faith, hope, and love.

Get ready for a wild ride. Hang with me as we spiral upward.

Chapter 2:
The Battles Begin

I love baseball! It's a part of my childhood that I look back on with fondness. An innocent time. Is there anything more American? I started playing early, at five or six years old, and quickly became a solid player. My father had a passion for the sport and my involvement in it. We spent hours working on my catching, throwing, and batting. He attended every game.

Just after I turned twelve years old, the Houston Astros let me work as a batboy for four games. Can you imagine a kid, that age, in love with a game, on the field with his favorite team and all his idols? I was in Heaven. I sat next to Jose Lima in the dugout as we sucked on sunflower seeds and flicked them forward. Jeff Bagwell paced the dugout in front of me but didn't offer as much camaraderie as Lima. Still, in my twelve-year-old mind, it was as if I was a part of the team. Lima died, tragically, just a few years later.

Needless to say, I lived and breathed baseball at this age and played on a number of select teams. I swung for the fences and became the first one to hit a ball over the fence in my age group. My best friend, Clayton, and his parents even came to some of my games. I cherish that time. When I took the field, my cares melted away. I only thought of smacking the ball deep into the outfield and rounding the bases. I appreciated the occasional pat on the shoulder and "good game" from those that came to watch.

As perfect as baseball was, an incident a few years prior shattered that perfect, middle-class, baseball life. A neighborhood friend, who was a year or two older, asked me to spend the night. I can't remember his name and don't want to remember it. The sexual abuse I endured that night didn't just scar me. It inflicted something much more powerful. A wound unseen. We all have markers in our lives, those turning points that dictate our direction. That road of light and dark. That new relationship. A new job. A death in the family. I didn't truly understand until a few years ago that the abuse became a marker for me to begin acting out. And my father would have none of my acting out.

My parents raised me and my sister, Brandy, in Houston, Texas, within suburbs called Richmond, Sugarland, and Missouri City. More people call Houston home than any other city in Texas, and it ranks fourth in the nation in population. I love the town I call home. Everything's bigger in Texas, and no city is larger in the state than Houston. A drive across town might take forty-five minutes or over an hour with moderate traffic. The city is named for Sam Houston, a hero of the Texas Revolution and the only person to serve as governor for two different states.

We Texans complain about the summer heat but really do love living in the Lone Star State. We're passionate about our barbeque and consume Tex-Mex once per week. The name Texas means "friend"—fitting, since we often gather for food, fun, and sports. It's in our blood. My parents certainly fit that stereotype, having spent all their lives here as well.

I'd love to tell you that I had perfect parents or that I was a perfect son. Neither is true. We lived in a safe neighborhood. I wore clean clothes and attended good schools. I never went without food. Nothing like that. They didn't have a lot of material things growing up and wanted something better for us.

My father had it much rougher in his neighborhood where race contributed to more than one fight. His father kept my dad and his two brothers hard-edged and had them duke it out if they had a conflict. Survival of the fittest. The fights could be brutal, and all three experienced the hard hand of my grandfather as well. One of those uncles committed suicide when I was three and the other is doing time for sexual assault. I don't really know him or much more about my dad's past. He's not interested in revisiting that part of his life.

My father is a hard worker. A skilled machinist. I remember him working the graveyard shift and waking me up to share Jack in the Box tacos. Good quality time. But his hard edge countered those few good memories. That acting out I mentioned above was typically met with a swift strike of his belt. I don't doubt that some of my misdeeds deserved appropriate, corrective discipline. As I aged a bit more, beyond twelve years old, he treated me differently. I can't explain it. The affection waned. If my bed wasn't made to standard, or if I looked at him funny, I felt his disdain.

I got the belt so often it didn't hurt anymore. One time I laughed at him after a weak strike on my backside. Huge mistake. I hate that our relationship devolved to only my misbehavior and his correction. He never spanked my sister to my knowledge so one might say they shared a different relationship, or maybe he thought the two genders required different methods of discipline. I've always wondered if some other measured way of handling my behavior would have given us better rapport.

I don't know how much my mother understood about these beatings. I always assumed she endured her own struggles. She tends to hold things in, and she spent a lot of time running a daycare center, so she didn't have much interaction with other adults. I remember her having bouts of depression. That had to have been hard because I know her as a loving person, but she and my dad are of one mind; that is, he typically takes the lead role. If he thinks a certain way, she'll typically follow suit.

Although they both have strong opinions on how we discipline our children, I don't think he'd ever strike my son. There's some sort of line he won't cross, and of course, I won't let him cross it. It may simply be that his father did it to him, and it's how he thinks boys learn.

I'm sure my father doesn't remember the frequency of these spankings. He might chalk it up to tough love, but they left an indelible impression on me. There may have been a degree of corrective discipline that would have actually benefited me at an early age. However, my child's brain thought the discipline unwarranted, so it had the opposite effect. It angered me. I only wanted to act out more. This was no short-lived phase. This was a battle that would rage for years. My anger drove me toward seeking comfort in things I thought would soothe the pain: cigarettes, alcohol, and drugs.

By the time I reached ten, I had seen my parents light up cigarettes thousands of times. Most kids experiment with their first smoke out of peer pressure or simple curiosity. Someone in the group scores a pack, and they find some secluded spot. They each light up. One coughs. One tries to act cool like they've done it before, and few admit how truly nasty it is the first time. You've seen it in a movie or TV show, or you may have done it yourself.

I truly thought smoking would heal my pain. I started by smoking leftover cigarettes from ashtrays that had enough tobacco left on them for a few drags. Sure, those first few grossed me out a bit, but I began to find pleasure in the nicotine. My dad smoked menthol, so his definitely offered a different experience. Soon, I began to steal one or two from their packs for later. They smoked enough that they didn't notice any missing. When I had the house to myself, I fired them up but never got caught because the house always smelled like smoke.

I began taking them to school and would smoke on the way home, influencing my friends to smoke with me. I was the one your mom warned you about. Okay, maybe there was a bit of co-influencing, but I absolutely was not the kid trying to stop us. At some point in those pre-teen years, I developed and then maintained a smoking habit.

At fourteen, my mom picked me up from school, and I hopped in the car. Her opened pack of Virginia Slims sat in the center console. Without saying a word, I picked up the pack, forced a cigarette out, and lit it up. I kind of expected her to say, "What do you think you're doing?" or to yank it from my mouth, but she said nothing. Just a look. I think she knew I had been smoking for some time. My grandparents had also let me smoke when I stayed with them. My mom ended up buying me my first pack, but I didn't smoke around my father until I turned sixteen. After that, I stopped caring what he thought.

My mom and dad are now ex-smokers. It took my mom a lot longer, but my dad quit in the only fashion you'd expect for someone so no-nonsense as him. He bought a carton and smoked one after another until it made him sick. Done! That's how he rolled.

That's how it started with cigarettes.

Alcohol is another story. It acted as a gateway into substance abuse unlike anything else I've done. Let me go ahead and declare that I'm an alcoholic.

"Hi, I'm Jason, and I'm an alcoholic" is something I've uttered many a time.

I have a sponsor and attend Alcoholics Anonymous. My struggles with liquor began at, you guessed it, an early age. I was eleven or twelve. You know, the same kid that had already been smoking.

I had watched my parents consume not only a ton of cigarettes, but alcohol too, almost every single day. Lots of beer. Tons of margaritas and the occasional mixed drink. They liked to have friends over or camp with other families, and alcohol always played a part. The grown-ups all seemed to enjoy drinking and have a great time. I thought it'd be fun. For my first real solo party, I stole a bottle of cinnamon schnapps from them and took it down to the creek. The party didn't last long. I got drunk alright, and sick as a dog as well.

"Yuck!"

Why would anyone like that? I thought.

As is the case with most who drink booze, my distaste was short-lived. On those camping trips, my friends and I waited for the parents to pass out and then sneak a few beers from the cooler. I soon learned to maximize the potential of this new way to escape life. I liked getting drunk.

My dad often took me offshore fishing. From our home southwest of Houston, we could drive to the Gulf of Mexico in a little over an hour. Once out on the water, I usually got seasick, but I enjoyed those trips with my father and the other friends that joined us. As you can imagine, coolers full of beer played their part. His friends laughed as they watched me steal my father's beer and down them without getting caught.

I can't pinpoint when my drinking became a problem. Of course, any kid drinking is a problem, I get that, but I mean when did it reach the stage where I had a "drinking problem"? During my middle school years, I looked for opportunities and took them. Parents out of the house. On a fishing trip. Camping trip. By my freshman year of high school, I drank from Thursday through Sunday. A weekend drunk fest. I did it so often, I don't really remember weekends when I wasn't drunk.

This seems like another good moment to pause because you may be thinking I'm full of it. You may be saying: This can't be true. No one that age drinks and smokes with reckless abandon. He's exaggerating.

I wish I was. I really do. But, I'm not.

My co-conspirators and I scored most of our libations at the gas station near our school where a few winos hung out. I know that's not a nice word—wino. They may have been homeless and in desperate need of help, but wino is how we thought of them at the time. Willing participants in our mischief. Our suppliers. We'd give them cash for a case of beer, followed up by a few cans for their effort. Sometimes we drank what they wanted. Mad Dog 20/20, Boone's Farm, anything cheap to get us drunk. We'd take our score to an abandoned barn near the school or a friend's house and drink away.

Since I drank so much on those Thursday nights, I skipped school a lot of Fridays. I don't know how much my parents knew about my weekend activities during those years. What they would have or could have done about it. We had no cell phones in those days, and I rarely returned their page requests. At some point, they had to know. The day they found me on a Sunday afternoon passed out drunk in the bushes outside our home surely disgusted them. It certainly disgusts me today.

My dad thought I'd end up dead and had this fear I'd be kidnapped. He came home late one night and woke me at 2:00 AM. We struggled as he held me firm.

"This is how easy it is to snatch a child," he said.

Bizarre—I know—how he connected all those dots, but his message was clear. You're going to get killed or kill yourself. Considering all the factors, it was sage advice. I was a cigarette-smoking, binge-drinking teen with no respect for my parents. But wait, there's more!

"Hi, I'm Jason and I'm an addict."

Yep, there are drugs too. Lots of drugs. Loads of 'em. I'm an addict that tried them all, and it started at the ripe ol' age of eight.

In the early 1990s, the diagnosing of children with ADHD (attention deficit hyperactivity disorder) was all the rage. Parents worried as teachers rattled off reports about children who were unable to focus, follow instructions, complete assignments, or interact socially. Sometimes there's an element of restlessness. To combat ADHD, Ritalin became the drug of choice.

Another parent or teacher would say, "You should get him on Ritalin."

In 1993, my mom felt I had ADHD and sought the drug.

No doubt, at that point in my life, I had been given typical over-the-counter medications to treat a cold, for example, or an antibiotic due to an ear infection. A doctor prescribed Ritalin for me to treat, not a passing condition, but a brain disorder. Treat doesn't seem the adequate word. Treat denotes a cure. Control is more like it. Ritalin can control the symptoms of ADHD, but there's no known cure.

Like any drug, Ritalin has loads of side effects. The typical ones, as with most medications, are nausea, trouble sleeping, headaches, etc. It can also cause twitching or uncontrollable tics. That's the one that got me almost immediately. People thought I had Tourette's syndrome. My tic looks as if I have the hiccups: I breathe in and make an audible noise. It occurs about once an hour. I say it occurs, as in the present tense, because I still have this tic today from that medicine I took as an eight-year-old. Fun, huh?

And, thus began a lifelong love-hate relationship with drugs. The legal and illegal kind. The over-the-counter and the controlled-substance type. Pills, powder, smoke, you name it. To be clear, I think my mother simply wanted to help me focus on my schoolwork, as did many of the mothers of kids I attended school with. It was the thing to do.

As I mentioned earlier in this chapter, about that marker in my life where I began acting out, not knowing about it, my parents thought my acting out had to do with issues of the mental variety. We'll fully explore that in the next chapter. For now, suffice it to say, my dad didn't "spare the rod," but my mom thought medication offered the best solution. At about twelve years old, my doctor prescribed me Trazodone, primarily used to treat depression. In essence, this drug makes you feel better. Improves your mood. Jumpstarts your day.

Well, I liked the Trazodone! Bunches. I liked it so much, I'd take five, six, or even seven to get high when I should have taken only one. The drug abuse went on for some time. I knew I'd eventually get caught, but the addict doesn't care. They only care about the next high. My parents busted me, which wasn't too hard since they noticed how fast my prescription ran out. My father locked up the drugs, but like the industrious addict I was, I found the key. This is one of those markers in my life.

After that, I knew how to get a feeling that cigarettes couldn't come close to and that alcohol sort of came close to. Drugs did the job so much faster. From cigarettes and alcohol to prescription drug abuse. See where this is going?

I know my parents disagreed on the medication. My dad once broke his foot and couldn't walk but still would not take his pain medication. He medicated with alcohol. As we move along in the story, we'll find that my mom, my dad, and my friends all developed skewed views on drugs and alcohol, with a flawed morality. I hope to correct that as someone who has experienced the worst from those substances and done the worst to others because of those substances.

At the same time as my Trazodone misadventures, I befriended Rick in middle school. A year older, he had a little more experience than me in the world of drugs. One time, when his parents left for a movie, he introduced me to marijuana. He didn't have to teach me to inhale, and the smoke didn't cause me to cough; I had all that experience from cigarettes. He did teach me how to hold the inhale for the best effect. Needless to say, we got baked! Please know, I'm not glorifying this, just showing you the gory details, so to speak. We cracked up at the littlest things, had the munchies, all that. Rick and I hung out a lot and smoked all the time.

How do middle school kids get access to and pay for marijuana? Great question.

We lived in a middle-to-upper-class neighborhood, so the kids had money. The drug dealers knew that. Simple supply and demand. It happened much later, after we had moved on to high school, but the police arrested one of our teachers for selling pot. My family didn't have the kind of money where the kids could blow serious funds without accountability to their parents. I mowed a bunch of lawns, earning as much as $200 per month. That's serious cash for a teenager. I didn't need to purchase whole bags or roll my own at this point. I could easily get three joints for $10 and did so on a regular basis.

One trait I have from my father is that of being a hard worker. I've never shied from that and will work my tail off, for others or myself. I sacked groceries at Randalls grocery store to add to my mowing money. Cash for drugs never became an issue. I soon needed extra funds to buy the latest craze—Ecstasy. It's both a stimulant and psychedelic that boosts the central nervous system and causes hallucinations. The user boasts of the euphoria. The thesaurus adds euphoria next to words like pleasure, happiness, cloud nine, dancing, laughing, well-being, and excitement. Ecstasy can also kill you by causing wild swings in body temperature. As I entered high school, Ecstasy made an appearance at every party.

I know that I enticed many to do drugs. Rather than purchasing a few rolled joints at a time, I began buying bags of the stuff and rolled dozens of joints. I bought, shared, and encouraged a ton of pot-smoking and alcohol-drinking.

I'm not in any way saying I had a ton of enablers around me but following is one example. A friend of my father's had a son who was in the penal system for most of his life. I became a surrogate son for him, and he'd take me on day trips where the beer and pot flowed, and no one gave a second thought to my consumption. I suppose if he had his son during those times, he would have influenced him to abuse those substances as well.

I did have people in my life that attempted to sway me another way. I loved spending time with my grandparents. I wouldn't call my grandfather perfect by any means. He certainly had issues, but I think he took them out on my father. He thought I walked on water and treated me really well. I didn't feel the need to abuse substances as much around him.

When I had a really tough time at home, my friend Chris's house became a refuge. His parents always greeted me with a smile and seemed genuinely glad for me to be there. Similarly, my buddy Clayton lived two streets over and let me stay often. With his family, I attended church on a regular basis for the first time. I didn't know much about Jesus or had the relationship with Him I needed to, but one could say the introduction began there. Seeds had been planted.

I'm sure some church folks, not understanding their own faith, may have found me quite unredeemable. Had I known only a little of the Bible, I'd have probably thought the same, but I did know that God provided an answer, even for people like me. God continually put people in my life that told me the opposite. I may not have listened then or understood, but they watered those seeds. As Paul taught, "I planted, Apollos watered, but God gave the growth. So neither he who plants nor he who waters is anything, but only God who gives the growth" (1 Cor. 3:6-7). I'm so thankful for the dozens of people God used to plant and water in my life.

This may seem like a beat-up-my-parents manifesto, but that's not my aim. The 1983 film *Bad Boys*, starring Sean Penn, has a scene where he's entering juvenile detention and sees a sign prohibiting smoking. He looks around and sees most of the other inmates smoking anyway. Were they incorrigible? Was I?

I'm sure I was quite the handful for any parents to deal with. I'm sure many times they pointed to the no smoking, no drinking, no drugs, no whatever sign, and I simply looked back, ignoring them.

Phew! That's a lot, I know, yet another thread of disease and turmoil, which ran through my whole teen years, requires its own chapter. It upended my life as much as all the other messes I've already shared. Turn the page.

***

(Note: At the end of each chapter, Kristyn will share some thoughts on how she's experienced this part of the story).

From Kristyn:

Jason and I grew up in similar circles of suburban Houston. Like other Texas kids, we spent our summers by the pool and winters hoping it would snow, but it rarely did. Although my mom and dad didn't stay married, I'm thankful to have had a relationship with them both. That can be a tough thing growing up. I stayed with my mom most of the time in a middle-class neighborhood. So, Jason and I had much different childhoods regarding home life, but our surroundings were similar.

Like most teens attending high school parties, I had seen my share of people drinking, maybe sneaking off to do some sort of drug in a bathroom or driving off to a secluded spot. It wasn't really my thing, but it didn't shock me either. When I met Jason, I focused on him as a person rather than on what he had done in his sixteen years of life. As he started to reveal more and more of his past, I began to say to myself, "Surely, there can't be more." Well, there was more. A lot more.

I could see that he was a partier, but at first, it didn't seem like too much. In reality, we were spending so much time together that he had backed off from much of that. We spent most of our time talking and getting to know one another rather than partying. As we talked, he told me more about his drinking habit. *Okay, he likes to party.* That's pretty normal for a teenager in our hometown. Then, I learned he had been drinking for years. That was one layer. I watched him smoke without spending much thought on it. Then he revealed that he'd smoked since he was twelve. He added in smoking marijuana, and I realized it was yet another layer.

How big was this onion? Any more layers?

I certainly wasn't some angel myself and didn't think of him in some judgmental tone, but rather, I wondered what kind of person I was getting involved with. One thing about Jason is that he treated me incredibly well. So sweet. So gentle. I loved that. He didn't seem dangerous to me, but I wondered if he might be living dangerously. I wasn't one of those girls looking for the bad guy, but I must admit that all those layers intrigued me and scared me at the same time.

The part of his past that really concerned me was how he had endured his father's discipline. Jason would admit he deserved plenty of punishment, but that it sometimes occurred for no reason at all. He became immune from the result of punishment, that is, the punishment meant nothing. It wasn't corrective, but he had to take it and move on. When he spoke about this, I could almost see the pain in his eyes. The hurt. It made me both sad and mad at the same time. I wondered if that had caused all the drinking and drug abuse.

When it came time to meet his parents, I was nervous. I wanted them to like me. I was the first girl he had ever taken home. I thought they might just chew me up and spit me out. To say that the first night at his home was awkward would be an understatement, but I ended up bonding with his sister, and that smoothed over a lot of the tension. I soon became very comfortable with them but wondered how much Jason's parents knew about his extracurricular activities.

Their philosophy on discipline would conflict with ours once we had kids. I had to balance between respecting my elders and practicing the discipline I thought best reflected our belief system. Over time, I've realized that we didn't have perfect parents, and Jason and I certainly aren't perfect parents. I do count myself blessed with the parents I have and try to model much of what they taught me in the way I treat my kids. I love being a wife, but I consider my role as a mother one of the greatest callings God could have given me.

Chapter 3:
The Downward Spiral

My parents are huge horror film fans, especially the slasher flicks. They named me Jason after the main antagonist in the *Friday the 13th* films. The Jason in the film dies from drowning due to the negligence of camp counselors, so a distraught mother seeks revenge on future camp counselors. Spoiler alert. Sorry.

Don't worry, this isn't the part where I suggest that Jason (or his mother) are misunderstood and justified in the ingenious and varying ways they murder camp counselors while staying in cabins. I think it's a funny anecdote that they named me after him, but it allows me to reiterate the point that I realize some will seek to justify every bad decision or bad thing that they do. That's not my intention here. I own most of it, but it's my sincere belief that other forces can nudge us along.

I suffer from an ugly and cruel disease known as bipolar disorder. It's one of those things that most don't see. No one notices this physical ailment I'm struggling with; I wear no sign to announce. It's just there, wreaking havoc on my mind and my family. It affects those afflicted with the disease differently, but common symptoms are trouble sleeping, as in staying up for days on end. A mind racing so fast that it's difficult to hold a cogent thought. This lack of control over one's thinking can cause impulsive thoughts and actions such as drinking, online shopping, promiscuity, and drugs. Sufferers might have difficulty holding a conversation because they bounce from one subject to another. Mood swings can range from depression, to euphoria, or to rage in an instant.

There are many myths about this disorder such as its rarity among the population, but the National Institute of Mental Health estimates that it affects 4.4% of the population. Many believe children don't get it, and that it only manifests in adults, but it can run alongside other ailments such as ADHD from a young age. Much of the public's understanding is on the depression side of bipolar disorder, but the manic phase produces a great threat to many and can be far worse than the depression. Drugs and alcohol don't cause this disorder, but they can greatly exacerbate it as sufferers attempt to medicate themselves through those means.

It's possible that bipolar disorder more closely described what ailed me as a kid than ADHD. Although I had many ADHD symptoms, my mind also darted in a dozen directions. It wasn't only lack of focus, but wild swings with fits of anger (mania). I raged at things. I certainly acted out like any kid, but I displayed more hyperactivity. The Ritalin helped calm my mania to some extent but it also gave me a euphoric state. In essence, it made me high. I loved that part. In addition to the tics I mentioned in the last chapter, another side effect I experienced occurred most often during baseball when my heart raced and felt like it would explode out of my chest.

Looking back now, I may have been both misdiagnosed and taking the wrong medication. I don't say it that way to point fingers or blame my mother or doctor. I state this so that we consider whether children who are diagnosed with ADHD or simply having discipline problems might have something else going on.

In a nutshell, I had a lot going on, but one thing surpassed all others—rage!

At twelve years old, so many things seemed to anger me. Toward the end of that summer, I met some friends in a field to throw the football around. One kid did something that set me off. The argument escalated to a fight that didn't end well, physically for him, and legally for me. Weeks later, the principal pulled me from class. The police were waiting. They slapped handcuffs on me and delivered me to juvenile detention. I wasn't exactly headed toward being voted class favorite.

At that age, with my medium build, I was no bigger than the other kids or than the one that bore the wrath of my anger that day. I didn't go out of my way to bully. I simply lost control of my temper. I didn't have a tough-guy image in the slammer. Jail scared me as it would most that age. At one point, they placed me in a holding cell with kids three or four years older. I feared for my life as all of them towered over me.

I spent most of my time in a single cell for my protection while the big kids watched television in the dayroom. They gave me a Bible, and we had access to other books. It's there that I fell in love with reading. I first looked at the Bible and maybe read a few passages but had no concept of what I was reading. In Christian circles, we often talk of hiding God's word in your heart. I don't know what specifically was hidden in my heart, but I'm sure some of His wisdom found its way into my conscience. My family never went to church, but when I stayed with my friend Clayton, his family's talk certainly matched their walk, and they loved on me when I was unlovable. Or, at least, I thought I was unlovable. A perennial troublemaker. The more I read the Bible, the more I remembered things Clayton's parents had said or things I had heard in church. I didn't know it at the time, but God had begun to work on me. He was always there, but He began to reveal more of Himself to me. There began a journey, but it would take me three years to take more profound steps.

My parents visited often. My mother cried a lot, and I think my father pondered over how to fix the situation. About three weeks later, a psychiatrist officially diagnosed me with bipolar disorder with violent tendencies. I don't know if my parents were relieved to receive a more succinct diagnosis or mortified that a doctor stated, out loud, that I had a mental illness. A judge sentenced me to six years' probation, and the doctor ordered medication. I gave no argument to these daily pills because I loved the high. I loved it so much I'd take five or six rather than the prescribed one—the Trazodone I mentioned earlier. This is one of those markers in my life. Another decision that caused the downward spiral. The drug abuse went on for some time. I knew I'd eventually get caught, but the addict doesn't care. They only care about the next high. Once my parents found out, my father again locked up the drugs, but I quickly defeated the lock.

Once I was freed from juvenile detention, the school district feared my presence amongst the other students and transferred me to an alternative school. The incident carried a felony charge, but the authorities would later drop it to a misdemeanor. I didn't think of myself as a danger to society, but they sure did.

In this behavioral learning center, I spent my days in quiet, seated at a desk that had partitions enclosed around me. There was no talking, no recess, and no teaching. I ate my lunch in silence. In the past, I had made solid As and Bs in school and liked English and History. Teachers sent more assignments as I completed what I could, but I learned little in that environment.

The isolation continued at home. Due to my house arrest, I didn't see my friends. The boredom and listlessness took their toll. This seemed a life sentence to me. A never-ending gloom. An eternity. I wanted it to end and could think of only one way out.

For several days, thoughts of suicide welled up in me. One day I determined to end the suffering. I waited for my parents and Brandy to fall asleep. I walked into my closet, pushed the clothes aside, tied a belt around the hanger rod and then around my neck. I didn't hesitate. I just did it.

I'd like to tell you what thoughts went through my head at that moment. I cannot really remember. I didn't pray. I didn't cry. I don't think they'd resemble anything coherent. The rambling thoughts of a hopeless kid. I only sought an end.

Crack!

The hanger rod broke, waking my parents. They rushed in and found me alive but unwell. I didn't do any physical damage, but they couldn't deny the mental damage. They immediately checked me into a psychiatric hospital. I'll pause now to tell you that this span of a few months began years of trips in and out of juvenile detention and psychiatric hospitals. Some of these stays are blurred, but specific memories are clear.

Inside this hospital, the locked doors, the serious adults, and the strange looks from my fellow captives reminded me of juvenile detention. However, a small part of me felt like I needed to be in that hospital. I knew a sickness ravaged my mind, and I hoped for some cure. I didn't want to be like that. Sure, I wanted the high from the drugs. I wanted to smoke cigarettes and sneak my dad's beers. But I hated the mania. I took no pleasure in it. There was no decision. No choice. An addict worries little about the lack of control they have, or the ramifications, as they're taking their drug. They're only consumed with the high. With mania, the lack of control is certainly there, with all its ramifications.

For many, the depression side presents such a dire state that suicide seems like the only answer. Imagine a ravaged mind at twelve years old, contemplating this dilemma. Whether depression or mania, an evil overtakes the mind. Scripture tells us that "the devil prowls around like a roaring lion, seeking someone to devour" (1 Peter 5:8b). I felt so helpless. Easy prey. The Enemy most assuredly had a field day with me during this time.

Someone could legitimately ask, "What were you thinking?"

My answer would be, "Think?"

I wasn't the one thinking. Not completely, that is. My thoughts began with me, but without constraint, spun wildly out of control. That's life with bipolar disorder. Chaos. Prey.

When many heard of musician Chris Cornell's death by suicide, I'm sure they thought, "Huh, another musician meets a tragic end." Of course, his occupation had nothing to do with his problems. He'd abused drugs and alcohol from an early age and battled depression. He'd done the rehab thing, but something finally overtook him that was so powerful, he couldn't see any other way out. That's the work of the Enemy. Seeking to devour.

The hospital released me after two weeks and changed my medication. We all hoped for the best. The school system put me right back in the alternative school, and I returned to abusing my drugs. I felt like I had returned to square one. Nothing had changed. Back to the confinement and desolation. After a couple of months, I made my second attempt at suicide by taking an entire bottle of pills. The medical staff saved my life by pumping my stomach, and I found myself back at the psychiatric hospital. My dad always had great insurance, so a cycle of ten to fourteen hospital stays became the norm. For those keeping score, before I turned fourteen, I smoked like a chimney, drank beer, abused medication, committed a felony, and had made two suicide attempts. My parents must have been so proud.

The conversations with psychiatrists always sounded the same.

The doctor would peer over their glasses. "What is your mood, Jason?"

I'd shrug. "I dunno. Okay, I guess."

"What are your goals for today?"

"Hang out. Watch TV," I'd say, shifting in my chair.

"That's it. Can you think of something more productive?"

I'd look to the side, pretending to think. "Be positive. Read."

That's all I'd normally say. I really wanted to say, "My goal is to get out of this place. It's all I think about."

However, I wasn't in as big a hurry to leave the hospital this time. I met a girl there. A patient, like me, but a little older. She schooled me in my first sexual experience, causing a welcome distraction to my stay. I'm not saying this was a positive or appropriate action, but it explains why I did what I could to stay institutionalized that stay. As my doctor talked me out of thoughts of suicide, I convinced him that I very much wanted to take my life. A ruse for more drugs and more time with my new friend. For years, I became a master at telling doctors and counselors what they wanted to hear or what I needed to tell them to accomplish my mission.

While some of the treatments probably helped, the cure was temporary. A Band-Aid on a gaping wound. It's difficult to treat someone so apathetic. Nothing doctors, counselors, or my parents said mattered to me. My focus remained on getting high or giving up on my life. That girl only served as a temporary high. "For out of the abundance of the heart the mouth speaks" (Matthew 12:34). How true! Oh, man, the things that came out of my mouth. Things like, "I don't care," or "Screw it," to name a few. That was my heart. My true nature at that time. I had no spiritual bearing. I had no guiding light. Just anger, resentment, and indifference.

I only fooled them for a few weeks. Upon this release, things changed slightly. With the felony charge reduced, the school let me back with my classmates. I expected them to distance from me or ask a million awkward questions, but they treated me as if nothing had happened. My dad did a better job locking up and/or hiding my medication, but I still managed to sneak a few more than needed and got high. Seventh grade came to a close with no further incidents. But that was just seventh grade.

Before long, another assault charge reared its head, but it had no foundation. To this day, I don't understand why that person leveled the charge, but the police sided with them. I was on the wrong side of a bad reputation. Back in juvenile detention, I stayed for two weeks until they dismissed the charges after learning the truth. Once you're branded as a "troubled" teen, people will assume the worst. The new school year had started rough, but thankfully, no one knew why I had missed a couple of weeks.

I know none of this was easy for my parents. I can't imagine how many times they threw their hands up in the air. Quite frankly, they could have simply given up on me, but they kept trying to find me the help I needed. That doesn't mean fireworks didn't explode between us. There were plenty of those incidents. One time as we rode home from dinner, I had a huge argument with my father. I can't even remember the subject, but as he rolled to a stop, I hopped out of the car. He drove off with my mother and sister. I arrived home after nearly three hours of walking. I always made it back home somehow. I always found my way home. I never really cared about disappointing or angering them, but I did care about my father's belt at that age, so I walked a fine line between a verbal dressing down and corporal punishment.

As you might imagine, I missed a ton of school. My studies always came easily to me, so I'd manage to catch up. When I wasn't locked up, I'd skip school a lot or feign sickness and spend the day with my mom at her nursing-home job. I'd do odd jobs there, and her boss would sign off on the right documents for me to get some sort of school credit. I thought I was so clever then with my schemes and ability to wiggle out of responsibilities. I spent a lot of time with my mother. When she and my dad had problems, I lived with her at a women's shelter for a couple of days. She gave me that refuge I sometimes needed while she sought her own refuge.

Another element of probation, and perhaps a positive experience, was when they assigned me community service. I worked in a local animal shelter cleaning pens, as well as bathing and feeding dogs. I liked it so much, I asked for a paying job with them, and they let me stay. These animals gave me something to care for. It's no wonder that service dogs provide comfort to so many, and horses are being used to help with PTSD. The animals took my mind off those negative inclinations and gave me something positive to do with my life. Something to look forward to.

I returned to juvenile detention and psychiatric hospitals so many times over the next few years that I lost count. Continued suicide attempts by overdose caused the hospital admissions, but I earned my stays in juvenile detention with a variety of offenses. I didn't always take more than my correct dosage just to get high; I sold them as well to kids at school. Due to my probation, I had to take regular drug tests and often failed them because of marijuana. They'd send me to juvenile detention for a few days, and I'd return to my old ways. At that point, it seemed like a slap on the hand. A ridiculous, yet vicious cycle.

After one particular failed drug test, they sentenced me to a few "motivation days," commonly called boot camp, since they simulated a military-like experience. They forced us to perform an array of strenuous exercises like pushups, situps, jumping jacks, and running. One day I had enough and announced, "I quit!" They had a response for my proclamation: hog-tying me by handcuffing my wrists behind my back, cuffing my ankles, and then pulling both to the center of my backside. I lay on my stomach, miserable, desperate, and out of control. And, it hurt. I begged them to release me, which they did, and I willingly returned to the exercise regimen. Aside from the first few days in juvenile detention, it was the only other time when I determined to do anything to keep from being locked up again.

God has always blessed me with great friends. Since I was typically the instigator, their parents offered me a lot of grace during those troubled days. At fifteen, I left home to hang out with my friend, also named Will. My probation required house arrest for anything other than school or work. Of course, that's the day my probation officer decided to come by for an impromptu visit. My sister, Brandy, called me at Will's house on the landline. We didn't have cell phones in those days. I knew I was busted but thought if I sprinted back to my house, it might look like I hadn't really left. Will joined me in the race, and we bolted through his back door.

A long, meandering creek connected our neighborhoods as part of a greenbelt behind the rows of homes. Several tiny bridges allowed pedestrians or motorists to crossover, and many enjoyed walking, running, and biking in those areas. Will and I weren't running for our health, though, we were running to keep me out of the clink—a scheme fraught with error. As we navigated those bridges, rocks, and puddles, I noticed a beautiful redhead walking with another girl.

If you've watched the scene in *Ferris Bueller's Day Off* where he's making a similar rush through his neighborhood to get back to his house but takes the time to introduce himself to two women, then you'll get the picture. We slowed our run to a jog and then stopped altogether. Will knew the girls and introduced me to them. Kristyn, the redhead, took my breath away. I forgot about the probation officer and any other coherent thought as she mesmerized me. After we all talked for a couple of minutes, Will reminded me that I really needed to get home. We said our goodbyes and sprinted toward my house.

I didn't fool my probation officer. Not even close, but he let me off with a warning. Thankfully I was sober at the time. I couldn't stop thinking about Kristyn. I dreamed about her night and day. We'd not meet again for a long time, but my life was changed that day for sure. It might be the only time I was thankful for my probation officer.

At fifteen, my weekends were blurred by drugs, alcohol, and the prescribed medication for my bipolar disorder. Of course, mixing these, or using the prescribed medicine with inconsistency, didn't help matters at all. As a result of the mania, I cannot sleep without medication. My mind races so much, I cannot relax enough to fall asleep. The medication regulates that. Without it, I'd stay up for days on end binging on booze or whatever drug is handy. My racing mind couldn't keep up with my thoughts and caused cravings for impulsive things like drinking or other stimulants. The higher I became, the more things made sense. Then I'd crash, blackout, and sleep for two days. I'd go to one extreme and then another.

A person with bipolar disorder can have such a hard time focusing or making sense of normal things, they have an overpowering temptation for pleasure. It leads many to promiscuity. I had some struggles with that but was locked up so much I never had a serious girlfriend until I met Kristyn.

Most of my life, I've taken drugs like Thorazine, Xanax, Gabapentin, and Adderall to control my affliction, regulate my sleep, and keep me on an otherwise even keel. Today, I'm extremely regimented with my medication, but back then, I stacked abuse on top of abuse.

One positive constant existed during that time—baseball. I played on one select team after another during those teen years despite all the interruptions. I tried football once, but mainly played that to help me bulk up. Between the violence of the sport and a dislocated finger, I chose to stick with baseball. My love for baseball stems from the same places it does for most. I like the history of the sport. Its connection to mom and apple pie. The summer pastime. The pace of the game. That, and my talent for the sport. I don't want this to come across as prideful, but baseball is one thing I was really good at it, if not great.

I played catcher, and only a rare, wild pitch made it past me. I learned to call pitches long before the age that most players start doing that. On the offensive side of the ball, I carried a huge slugging percentage. A big hitter with batting averages in the high .300s. My coaches assured me that great things awaited me. A college scholarship or even a shot in the Major League.

The idea of high school ball thrilled me. As a fifteen-year-old freshman, I made the varsity team. In the first game, I blasted a home run over the fence. It was glorious. Exhilarating. But something excited me more. I get it. This is the part of my story that should be a turning point, where the troubled youth finds freedom from addiction and mania through baseball. That would make a great film. Sadly, it's not mine. No, partying, girls, drugs, and alcohol all took first place in my life, and baseball meant regular drug tests. I worried that baseball would expose me. I had built a house of cards of decadence and didn't want it to come crashing down. That's how addicts think. Not how a high school kid with his whole life in front of him should've been thinking.

Most adults have that one high school regret. They wished they'd studied harder, asked that person out on a date, or stuck with a particular activity or sport. Quite abruptly, halfway through that freshman season, I quit baseball. Needless to say, the coaches, my parents, and my friends were dumbfounded. Why would Jason, with all that talent, give up a game he loves? they thought. The answer is, that's what addicts do. It's what irrational people do. I realize that I've focused on bipolar disorder in this chapter, but don't blame that for all of my actions. It's not something I gave myself through a stupid action. It just happened to me and affects so much of my life. I don't know how I got it. Some studies suggest that it's typically a hereditary disease, but that's not always the case. We do have people in our family who seem afflicted. It is a contributing factor, not the sole reason, for so many of my irrational actions, like quitting baseball.

With that great game gone from life, I did what I knew well. I partied. My friend group consisted of vastly different personalities, but we all got along. We camped a lot on the Comal River in New Braunfels, Texas, or took a road trip to the beach at Galveston. All those trips meant gallons of booze and whatever drug we had acquired. I wasn't thinking about my future. I was living day to day, party to party.

As my sixteenth birthday approached, I looked forward to that milestone, especially getting my driver's license. However, my actions began to converge toward one event that would alter my life physically and spiritually.

***

From Kristyn:

If I had polled my girlfriends during my high school years, asking whether they had a boyfriend that had done drugs or drunk alcohol, many would have answered yes. However, I don't know if any of them had a boyfriend with numerous stays in psychiatric hospitals. I must admit, that freaked me out a little.

Is this guy just wounded, or does he have something more severe going on? I thought.

He told me he had made a couple of suicide attempts. Most people might say they had made a suicide attempt. As in one. He said a couple. Could that mean several? I went from freaking out to feeling concern. I wanted desperately to go back and help that little boy.

If you're around Jason for a short period of time, you'll hear him make a sound like a hiccup. It's actually a tic. I certainly noticed it and asked him about this. He explained that it was a side effect from Ritalin he took for ADHD. That's something most people my age know about. It seemed a third of the students in my classes in elementary school took Ritalin. He then told me about his bipolar disorder. That was something I knew nothing about. He added words and phrases like "mania" and "racing mind." All this was foreign to me.

"You mean like depressed?" I asked.

He explained a little more, but I could only think about it as a mental illness. I wasn't judgmental about it; rather, I felt concerned for him. How hard it must have been for him to deal with that. I couldn't imagine dealing with all those highs and lows throughout the day. Today, I'm thankful he has good doctors and great medication to deal with this. I've seen him off his medications, where he's up all night with his mind taking him in a dozen different directions.

I don't know that I fully realized it then, but I certainly know now how much my faith in God helped me to deal with all that. His mental illness was truly an illness. The drinking and drug use didn't just happen to him. He was not born with it. He made those decisions and owns them. However, he was born with bipolar disorder. I know that only God can heal him of that. As the wife of someone struggling with that on a daily basis, I lean on my faith daily. Countless times I've worried that he might be having suicidal thoughts. That's something that has plagued him for his entire life. I'm thankful we share the same faith and count on Christ and Christ alone to fight that urge to give up.

When I was growing up, my family attended church on a regular basis, so I came to faith in Christ at a young age. As a believer in Jesus Christ, I go to Him, the Bible, and prayer in times both good and bad.

My father has modeled what it means to be a Christian in so many ways. I've turned to him many times for advice throughout my life. When he first heard some of the elements of Jason's life, he cautioned me about deepening my relationship with Jason. He probably wanted me to just run away from the relationship, but he tried to allow me some independence and the opportunity to make a mistake or two. Essentially, he let me have a life.

At this point, it may seem that all Jason and I did was talk about his past. That certainly wasn't the case. We talked about everything. We did all those normal things young couples do. We hung out with friends, saw movies, studied, and talked about the future. I loved watching him play baseball. It's a lot of fun when your boyfriend is one of the best players on the team. He had so much passion for the game. It disappointed me when he gave it up.

So, although this layer of his life concerned me, we reached the point where we knew each other pretty well and accepted one another's pasts. However, when he said he had "mania," I didn't really know what that meant and hoped I never had to witness it.

Chapter 4:
Locked Away

It's probably understandable, if not the next logical conclusion, that I'd find myself locked away for an extended period before I left my teen years. In *The Shawshank Redemption*, the character Red says, "I have to remind myself that some birds aren't meant to be caged," in reference to his friend Andy, who has just escaped. I look back on my sixteenth year of life and ponder that sentiment. Maybe I needed some cage time. An extended time-out, if you will.

A month past that sixteenth birthday not much changed. My smoking, drug use, drinking, and ill-temper remained. A dangerous cocktail—no pun intended. The same things that had caused my other stays in both juvenile detention and psychiatric hospitals culminated on one fateful day. Another incident in a long line of poor choices.

Four or five police arrived to restrain me. My rage had reached an unbearable level, the by-product of mania. The handcuffs were tight, but I'd worn them before. By the time they placed me in the back of the police car, I had calmed, but the damage was done. I knew I had really messed up. I knew they'd put me away for a long time. I was no longer a child, and I wondered if I'd just kissed my teen years goodbye.

They placed me in a padded cell that night, fearing I'd harm myself. It was a valid fear. Violence welled up in me to uncontrollable levels. The by-product of mania. Rubber foam lined the floors, walls, and ceiling, with a drain in the center to prevent flooding from the sink. I could have punched at the wall and banged my head but would have done no damage. All I could do was pace and ponder. I spent most of my time there that first week with nothing but my thoughts and a red-covered Bible. One book that had all the answers I'd ever need, yet I didn't know it at the time.

I'd open it to different places and read passages. The concepts weren't foreign to me. I'd recognize things I'd heard when attending church with Clayton. I didn't know it at the time, but God had begun to work in me through those church visits. He'd always been there before, but my heart began to open up. A door, slightly ajar, with me peeking out and God shining in. I don't remember the exact moment, but a couple of years before, I had made a decision for Christ. I was no theologian, but I understood the basic Gospel. I knew that I had sinned and could only find salvation in Jesus Christ. The childlike faith I had, drove me to prayer and daily Bible reading. However, I lacked complete commitment, and that fateful day, the adversaries of substance abuse and mania had done their evil work.

My mind raced, with ideas of getting high or taking my life, as well as with thoughts that fed a strange pull to do the right thing and clean up my life. So, I sat in the padded cell and read the Scripture. My mind had cleared some, because the state of Texas imposed cold turkey on me. No cigarettes. No alcohol. No illicit drugs. Only prescription medications to treat my condition. I'd occasionally press the intercom to be escorted for a toilet break but had no other contact with humans. After nearly a week, I appeared before a judge who knew me well. That's never a good thing.

"Jason, I've given you chance after chance. My hands are tied." She banged the gavel and ordered me to twelve months in juvenile detention.

I wasn't really sure what that meant. I'd been to jail before. I'd been to hospitals before. This sounded like jail.

Just a month after that milestone birthday—sixteen—and all the plans I had vanished. I'd spend that year locked up. They placed me in a different cell without padding as I awaited transfer to the long-term facility. I met with my parents, but we spoke few words. What could be said? My father said absolutely nothing, and my mother cried.

A police car transported me from the county jail to some unknown place. My fear increased at every turn down a different street. I had no idea what to expect. The fear of the unknown can sometimes cause us the greatest angst. Would they place me in solitary? Would other prisoners jump me? How would I survive a whole year without getting drunk or high? Yes, I had that concern.

My mom met me there with a few items they allowed. Those of us in there wore our own clothes, assuming they had no writing on them, and we could have some books. I had that red Bible they had given me, and she brought a few novels, *Angels and Demons* by Dan Brown among them. I had writing materials and a few CDs of my favorite bands, such as Limp Bizkit, Orgy, and Korn.

My new home wasn't exactly Alcatraz but, rather, a juvenile residential treatment center behind locked doors and tight security. The center, a collection of closely connected but not-quite-attached buildings, may have served some other purpose at one point. A tall fence lined the rear of the property. Hardly home sweet home.

My mom and I walked into a secured lobby as a disinterested guard buzzed me in. We exchanged final glances. I'd never seen her look so defeated. I walked past the day room, met with stares from those I'd soon share a lot of time with. Everyone seemed so cold to me, but I certainly didn't expect a warm reception. I noticed the heavy furniture and later learned it was designed that way so inmates could not use the items as weapons. As the guard removed my handcuffs, I noticed all the signs. Most of them were rules like "No Cussing" and "No Fighting." What I had struggled with in the past—rules—was something I now had to embrace.

Girls stayed on the first story with boys on the second and third. A man led me to the second floor and into my room, which I'd share with a rotating door of roommates. I had so many none of them stand out. They housed two of us to a room. We each had our own twin bed and dresser on carpeted floor and shared a bathroom. Every fifteen to thirty minutes, someone came around and counted us. That happened twenty-four hours a day, seven days a week. I settled in that first night and learned that lights out meant we were to go to bed. The door slammed shut, and I lay there wondering how I'd get through a year of that. No messing around. A strict schedule with no augmentation.

The lights came back on at 6:00 AM with screams to "Get up!"

It felt a little like I'd enlisted in the military, though it wasn't quite the banging of trash cans for an alarm clock. They gave us thirty minutes to get ready and ushered us to breakfast where we typically had eggs, bacon, pancakes, or cereal. Not exactly home cooking, but most of the meals were well-balanced, and I actually gained weight during my stay. We spent the first part of our morning with thirty to forty minutes of group therapy, some quiet time, and then school.

The boys, ranging in age from twelve to seventeen, shared one large schoolroom. There wasn't much, if any, lecturing, and the teacher just moved us along in our studies. Lunch came at noon with chicken tenders or sandwiches and then it was back to school. They allowed us an hour of recreation in the late afternoon. It was our only opportunity to get outside in the yard surrounded by that tall fence. We never ventured near the fence, a major rule violation. We were already locked up but certainly didn't want solitary. During that hour, though, most of us headed to the gym and played dodgeball or basketball. I typically played hoops and got pretty good but had to contend with a lot of dirty players. Competitors valued fouling and smack talk as much as ball skills.

We'd have more group therapy, or sometimes individual therapy, and then a dinner of tacos, hamburgers, or meatloaf. They diversified the selection with lots of veggies and red meat. I think the food kept us from getting too restless.

In the evening, we showered, did laundry, or spent time in the dayroom. With no TV, I read a lot, a habit I've never lost. I read everything I could get my hands on, but mostly novels.

They assigned us chores that mostly involved cleaning. The whole place smelled like disinfectant. We swept, mopped, vacuumed, scrubbed, and wiped every inch of the place on a daily basis, with a deep clean once per week. That included all the common rooms, but we had to keep our own rooms spotless. Hundreds of lights kept the building well-lit and exposed the slightest bit of dirt or grime. The daily grind kept us moving in many directions, but we always had time to think about what we missed, that is, our freedom.

After six weeks, a resident (inmate) earned a color code of red, yellow, green, or blue. The worst offenders had red, which meant they stayed in lockdown. A yellow code meant a judge or probation officer approved visitation privileges on Saturday, authorizing their parents to take them for four hours for something like a meal nearby. Those with green could go home for twenty-four hours and blue for forty-eight. I started on yellow and eventually earned green but an altercation bumped me back to yellow.

One of the guards took my electric shaving kit and gave it to someone else. I never learned why, but furious, I punched him in the forehead and broke my hand. They sent me to a padded cell for the night. Mania had not only contributed to why I was locked up but it exacerbated the problem. That is, a normal person would've handled the situation verbally—spoken to the guard's supervisor, or told their counselor. Not me. I reacted swiftly with violence. I realized I'd never get green again due to my temper and didn't even think about blue.

We all had problems. Serious problems. Addiction. Troubled home lives. Violent tendencies. Rage. A year after my stay, one girl attacked a guard, so they secured her with restraints. She later died. I don't know the cause, or whether there was negligence, but I do know that what might seem like a calm day in the juvenile residential treatment center could turn to violence in an instant.

Fights happened all the time. I experienced eight or nine during my time there. I only remember instigating one fight but knew that when challenged I had to fight back, or it would be open season on me. I'd be victimized daily if I showed any weakness. A survival-of-the-fittest mentality ruled the place. I never desired to fight and knew deep down that I should turn the other cheek, but I felt I had to maintain a reputation as one who'd stand their ground.

I had trained in kickboxing and mixed martial arts, so I typically won or at least held the attacker at bay until the guards arrived. Many of these fights meant lockdown, where they sent us to our rooms for a day or two. Anytime there was unrest, they locked us down. When talk of a natural disaster, like a hurricane, or an event like the World Trade Center attacks spread through the inmates, they locked us down before we became unruly.

Everything seemed to revolve around racial lines. Who we sat with at lunch. Whose team we were on for basketball. Who we befriended. Who we backed when a fight started. We tended to join a click that was segregated by skin color. A common rite of passage was jumping some other kid of another color so your group could ensure your commitment. The first guy to befriend me turned out to be a white supremacist. Isaac was a year older and gave me several lectures about hate and racism. He wasn't the only one like that. One of the white leaders shared several Bible verses with us, skewing them to support his racist rants. As much as I regret the time I spent with Isaac, I very much valued time spent with another person in that detention center, someone who would become one of the most important people in my life.

Chaplain George ministered to all who would listen. He worked there while earning his Ph.D. at Houston Baptist University. Since I had months of racial hatred under my belt, both given and received, I remained skeptical why this huge, black man asked to spend time with me in Bible study. He received special permission for me to study with him after lights out. He worked twelve-hour shifts, and we'd study late into the night. I probably should have been locked up long before, but I think God orchestrated this time with George when I needed it most.

We'd study with him in groups, but I became the only one willing to do the late-night study. I didn't care that I only got five hours of sleep because George intently focused on God's Word, and its application to me and him. He taught me how to meditate deeply on the Word and prayer. He saw something in me that no one else ever had. I had felt like a throwaway. A screw-up. A wasted life. George saw value. George saw a child of God.

The handful of times I had attended church with Clayton or another friend gave me glimpses of the Gospel. I had listened only a little, but it was enough to catch those ripples. George forced me to dig deep. We read whole books of the Bible and discussed how they correlated to other books of the Bible. He explained how Scripture could influence me during times of grief, joy, money issues, and when

I needed comfort. My faith remained far from complete, but I even thought I might have a future in ministry. I began to see George as a savior figure. Not Jesus or the Messiah, but rather one who could take young people headed for a life in prison or worse and turn them into God-exalting, people-loving, productive citizens.

We only saw the girls from the first floor on Sundays during church in the cafeteria. A local church brought in a team to lead us in worship; other times, they bussed us to an outside church where we sat in a special section. The adults kept a sharp eye on us. We weren't really dangerous to the public because most of the violence was about territory in the unit, but many would run if given the opportunity. The girls presented the greatest flight risk at the facility because they lived on the first floor, but at church, all of us could easily take off. I never considered running because I didn't really know where I'd go. Early on, I had resigned myself to the fact that my time was relatively short, and I simply needed to finish it.

While I had these polar opposite relationships in juvenile detention with the racist Isaac and the "savior" George, I looked forward to calls with my friend Chris, who had joined the Navy and was stationed in Norfolk in a support role for SEAL teams. He helped me realize I had a future after jail. I'd also call my parents. I didn't tell them anything about my new studies in faith with George. I assumed my father would dismiss the notion, but my mom probably would have thought it good for me. I just didn't think they'd care about that part of my life.

Ironically, I never found much value in the hours of therapy I endured. While that judge had sentenced me to twelve months of lock-up, her aim had been for me to heal under that therapy. Mostly women served as our therapists, and I think they likely did the best they could as we tuned out much of what others said. Sometimes group therapy could be quite the adventure. We had this one guy who constantly requested an exorcism. Another guy we called Lurch, because he looked like the big, goofy guy in the *Addams Family*, would say he had to get inside his own head so that he could talk himself through the day. They entertained us, but the vast majority of the time our group discussions bored us.

Most of us simply told the therapists what they wanted to hear. They seemed to ask the same questions I had been asked in the psychiatric hospitals.

"How do you feel?"

"Good," I'd reply.

"What are your goals for the day?"

I'd shrug and say, "Read a book."

They'd nod and go to the next person.

I don't condone that we didn't value the time or fully participate. I realize that therapy could have benefited me greatly, but at the time, I only heard blah, blah, blah. One can only answer the same questions in so many ways.

Individual therapy went about the same for me. They pushed and prodded, but I gave little. I didn't want to talk about the way my father disciplined me. I never trusted authority figures to help me with what I considered unfair treatment. I didn't want to talk about my addictions. I didn't really understand my bipolar condition. I mainly sat there and daydreamed.

Although I thought I had to serve my entire twelve-month sentence, I didn't know that my assigned probation officer had been doing an assessment on me every thirty days and speaking with the counselors at the facility. I remained in the dark, so when a counselor told me I was going home a few months early, I thought, "I'll believe it when I see it." I was suspicious of anything an adult told me. It's not as if I'd been a model prisoner, but I probably kept my nose much cleaner than most. I couldn't help but think all that time with George left an impression on him. I had been sincere in our Bible study. I wondered if he had put in a good word for me or, in some way, led the way to my early release. I knew I'd be headed home eventually, but the lingering question in mind was whether I'd choose the good path or continue doing the same stupid things. I simply didn't know what the future held.

We stayed in lockdown often after 9/11 as tensions remained heightened. All of us seemed agitated. Although we had limited news of what had happened and had seen no video footage of it, bits of information crept in. While our friends and family stayed glued to the coverage on the outside, their fear and uncertainty spread to us. Arguments broke out over little things. Fights ensued. I spent the majority of those last few days confined to my room.

I walked out on October 9, 2001. The ninth is significant in my life. Something always happens on the ninth. I don't know why, but God certainly uses the significance of numbers in His Word. Seven, twelve, and forty, for example.

No "Welcome Home" banner greeted me. Not that I expected that. I don't know that my dad even believed I should have been home yet. I know it thrilled my mom. Brandy gave me little more than a nod. I'm sure my presence concerned her since the last time I was home, police removed me in handcuffs with a crazed look on my face. The psycho brother. Not that I deserved a hero's welcome. I was probably lucky they even allowed me back home.

My parents spent the next couple of days trying to convince school officials to let me back in. Although this was the fall of my junior year, all that self-paced study had put me ahead of my peers. Although I describe so many struggles, academics were never one. Had I avoided the substance abuse, I have no doubt I would have been on the honor roll.

I spent a lot of my new freedom online in chat rooms. My dad wasn't too happy that I took up the phone line and these were the days of modems. I had a lot of catching up to do having been away from the internet for a year.

Besides my time with George, the greatest value of that time locked up was that it gave me a cooling-off period from smoking, drinking, and drugs.

I'd love to tell you that I made George proud. That I'd learned my lesson and planned to make my parents proud. I'd love to tell you all that. I chose another path.

Within two days, I ran off to live with my friend Joseph, who happened to be Kristyn's old boyfriend. Not only that, but I had dated Joseph's sister. A small group. Before long, I smoked, drank, and did drugs with friends—that familiar allure drew me in. I had always thought I'd live somewhere else once I got out. Anyplace other than with my parents. I knew that too much time with my dad could cause another outburst. The mania had too strong a control over me.

Joseph's father, more than even Joseph, wanted me to stay. He was a recovering alcoholic and attended Alcoholics Anonymous meetings. He acted as a father figure for me during that time, sort of taking over for George. They attended church, and I'd go with them. I lived two separate lives. One knew God's Word and wanted to grow spiritually. The other was distracted by my next high. A parable Jesus told in Luke 8 describes this perfectly:

> "A sower went out to sow his seed. And as he sowed, some fell along the path and was trampled underfoot, and the birds of the air devoured it. And some fell on the rock, and as it grew up, it withered away, because it had no moisture. And some fell among thorns, and the thorns grew up with it and choked it. And some fell into good soil and grew and yielded a hundredfold." As he said these things, he called out, "He who has ears to hear, let him hear." And when his disciples asked him what this parable meant, he said, "To you it has been given to know the secrets of the kingdom of God, but for others they are in parables, so that 'seeing they may not see, and hearing they may not understand.' Now the parable is this: The seed is the word of God. The ones along the path are those who have heard; then the devil comes and takes away the word from their hearts, so that they may not believe and be saved. And the ones on the rock are those who, when they hear the word, receive it with joy. But these have no root; they believe for a while, and in time of testing fall away. And as for what fell among the thorns, they are those who hear, but as they

go on their way they are choked by the cares and riches and pleasures of life, and their fruit does not mature. As for that in the good soil, they are those who, hearing the word, hold it fast in an honest and good heart, and bear fruit with patience.

I'm the thorns guy. Dozens and dozens of thorns.

I lived out of a suitcase for the next six months, more or less. I'd move back in with my parents for a few weeks but then go back to Joseph's or somewhere else as I prepared to turn seventeen. I had wasted so much of my youth in and out of facilities and most of my sixteenth year. Had someone said, "Haven't you learned your lesson?" My reply would have been, "Nope."

Deep down, though, I knew I needed to make something of my life. I'd graduate in eighteen months with society depending on me to be one of its productive members. Playtime was over.

***

From Kristyn:

One could imagine that we had an awkward conversation or two in the first few days of our relationship.

"So, what have you been doing since we met that first time?" I asked.

Jason shrugged. "You know. Hanging out. Playing video games. Spent a year in juvenile detention."

"Uh, excuse me. Wha—" My eyes wide open.

"Where should I begin?" Jason said.

Well, it wasn't exactly like that, but he eventually revealed to me what he did the majority of his sixteenth year of life. He detailed for me what he called "an incident caused by rage." I didn't understand it at the time but did later, as he explained his condition, being off his medication, and the culmination of a number of factors. He wasn't justifying it, only explaining it. I had a million questions about what that was like, being locked up. I don't think he really liked to talk about it because he certainly wasn't proud of it. He wanted to hang out and be like everyone else. But he wasn't like everyone else.

The first time I saw his mania lived out was when his friend played a prank on me and left me in a vulnerable position by taking my clothes when I was changing. I was upset, but when Jason found out, it enraged him. I wanted him to yell at the guy, but Jason took it to another level. I think all of us witnessing the event stood in shock. The friend, I was sure, would never do that again. Normal things that we might simply dismiss could really set him off. It's something, thankfully, he's learned to control.

We've talked many times about that part of his life where most teens were learning to drive or doing all those sixteen-year-old things. I hate that he missed that but it's what gave him the passion to want to help others as they're experiencing those same things at that age. He wants them to know the love of Christ above anything else. He also wants to speak directly to them as someone who has walked in their shoes. He wants them to know that their life story is not already written. One bad choice or a few bad choices doesn't define them. They have the opportunity to make productive changes and live a full and productive life regardless of their upbringing or other things affecting their lives—they can live a life free from addiction.

It's my passion as well to tell the parents of those teens, or the spouses of those people, who feel as though they've failed, that there is life after addiction. There is life with bipolar disorder. So many families are torn apart by these things, because each party feels as if they're on an island, all alone. In this day and age, so many resources are available, to help the person afflicted and the family that loves them. We've included a sample in the appendix. I'm not saying it's easy, but I can attest to how God has seen us through this.

I love God's promise in the book of Isaiah. "Fear not, for I am with you; be not dismayed, for I am your God; I will strengthen you, I will help you, I will uphold you with my righteous right hand" (Isaiah 41:10).

I'm thankful Jason has had friends with parents that let him sleep on the couch and took him to church. They saw his faults but knew he needed God more than ever during these times. I'm thankful for George mentoring Jason. It's my prayer that others will have that person, someone willing to speak truth into their lives. Jason didn't right the ship overnight, but he's now in a position to speak that truth into the life of that scared sixteen-year-old locked away with no hope for the future.

Chapter 5:
I Star You

Amidst the chaos, God granted me a gift of unimaginable joy. I mentioned crossing paths with a cute redhead in a previous chapter as I rushed home to meet a likely irate probation officer. Although smitten with her at the time, I wouldn't find her again for more than a year. She went on with her life, and I went on with mine. Little did I know that a chance meeting on a walking path would alter the course of the rest of my life.

Free of juvenile detention, my "extracurricular" activities kept me too busy for girlfriends. I had focused on joining the Marine Corps and worked out relentlessly, dropping about ninety pounds in three months. If I met someone, great, if not, cool. I connected with those that could relate to what I'd been through. Not an enabler, nor someone to feel sorry for me, but someone that recognized my chaos as the struggle it was and wouldn't be scared off.

I looked a bit different than I had the previous year. While hanging out at a friend's house, the cute redhead walked in with a friend. I recognized her immediately. She didn't recognize me but wanted to meet me. A friend reminded her that we had already been introduced on the walking path that day. It's not exactly a spoiler, but we've been together since the ninth of April 2002. There's that lucky number nine again.

We sat on a couch, talked, kissed, and repeat. We skipped school the next day and had breakfast at Kroger. Classy date, right? We simply couldn't stop talking, sharing things from our pasts and plans for our future. Many reading this will remember meeting their significant other and staying up all night talking. You didn't want the night to end, but morning came. That was us. She was perfect. There was never a point where we formally agreed to be in a committed relationship. It simply happened.

We fell in love and spent nearly every day together. We'd have lunch together at school and meet after class. I had moved back home and often walked my dog to her house. I'd throw rocks at her window to get her attention so we could talk, and I could kiss her goodnight. I wanted to spend every waking moment with her. I asked her to the prom, and we looked forward to that big night. When it came, we camped out on a friend's living room floor with several others. We held each other and talked for hours. It was one of the best nights of my life.

She eventually knew everything from my past. The good, the bad, and the ugly. It came out slowly. Not that I hid anything, but there was so much to tell and so much of it sort of runs together. Due to my infatuation with her, I had cut back on my partying. I wanted to separate from the friend group we hung out with. I worried about things they said about Kristyn. Inappropriate things. She didn't really know about that and liked our group. She was enjoying our time with them until a friend played that prank on her and she saw my rage unleashed. She saw it firsthand that day as I dealt with the friend. It scared her because she saw a side of me she'd never seen.

My living situation hadn't improved, and I looked for alternatives. One friend's couch followed another until Kristyn's mom let me stay with them. She made Kristyn sleep in the master bedroom with her. Her parents had divorced and her father, Randy, lived elsewhere. When he found out, he was none too pleased. He chased me down the street with my own baseball bat. This sounds bad, but it was more of a comical scene. In retrospect, he probably handled that much better than I would have. He controls his temper much better than I do.

I didn't know where to go, but once again, a friend lent me their couch. A few days later, I walked to a local park to clear my head. I sat there contemplating my future and thought of Kristyn. I missed her and wanted to be with her. Randy happened to drive by and saw me.

He stopped and rolled down the window. "Do you really love my daughter?"

"Yes, sir. I do."

He nodded. "Then hop in. Let's go talk."

We went to Chilis, and had dinner plus a few beers. He shared a ton from his past, difficulties he experienced with his father. As it turned out, we shared much in common. Once I told him about my past, he opened his home to me. I'm sure that allowed him to keep an eye on me, but he genuinely wanted to make sure I had a roof over my head too. Kristyn and I had periods where we were forbidden to see one another, or periods where I stayed with a friend, but we still managed to get together. Defying adults didn't really bother me, but it petrified me for Randy to find out. I didn't want to let him down. I had begun to develop a deep respect for her father.

Kristyn's parents invited me over for dinner one evening, and we enjoyed some delicious chicken parmesan. We traded "yum" sounds and made small talk. Halfway through dinner, her father's demeanor changed from one of joy to sternness. He kept looking at me.

Did I say something? I thought.

Kristyn looked over at me, clearly wondering the same thing. Then she saw it. The cause of her father's distaste. I had a huge hickey on my neck. Kristyn hoped he hadn't and wouldn't notice.

As we finished dinner, he said, "Can I see you two outside?"

We stepped out on the front porch and he asked why I had the huge red mark on my neck.

I stammered. "Uh, I got bit by a mosquito." Some brilliant, quick thinking on my part.

He scoffed. "I may have been born at night, but it wasn't last night." He then proceeded to deliver a lengthy lecture.

We eventually earned the right to stay together although I'm sure he knew we had been seeing each other in secret anyway. Randy and his wife, Susan, knew that we were meant to be, as they say, and finally relented on any attempts to keep us apart. From that point, we stayed together in one place or another. After high school graduation, Kristyn started attending junior college and eventually gained acceptance to the

University of Houston. My father had helped me get a job in a machine shop, and I earned enough for my own apartment. Although Kristyn had a dorm room, she spent most of her time with me.

After a couple of years, I began working for Randy in his SERVPRO restoration business. He had us working temporarily in New Orleans after Hurricane Katrina while Kristyn worked at the office in the Houston area. Randy and I spent a lot of time together, so asking him to lunch was nothing out of the ordinary. I told him that I really needed to speak to him. In the car, he kept talking about this job and that job. I looked for my moment to break in, like a little kid jumping off the diving board for the first time.

I interrupted. "Randy. I really need to ask you something."

He paused.

"I want to ask for permission to marry your daughter." I put it out there as simple as that. He could have made me wait for several uncomfortable minutes before responding. Or said, "You do, huh?" But he didn't.

"Yes, of course," he replied with no hesitation.

It was that easy. I thought he would say yes, but I didn't want to take it for granted. I planned a surprise trip home for the weekend. I had my oldest and closest friend, Mike, and his wife invite Kristyn to ride with them to meet other friends to go on a party bus. They took her to a site called the Waterwall in Houston. She knew something was up as soon as she saw my truck. I had done a terrible job hiding it.

I walked up to her, dropped to one knee, and opened the velvet-lined box holding the engagement ring. Pretty slick, huh? As I pulled it from its slit, the ring flew out and headed for a grate. One bounce. Two bounces. All four of us made a mad rush to save the ring and, thankfully, kept it from disappearing. Not a great start. I asked, and she said, "Yes!" We all cried and hugged. But the surprises weren't over yet.

We went to dinner at McCormick and Schmick's in Houston—an upscale steak and seafood place. Both our families were there to celebrate. The restaurant even had menus that said, "Congratulations, Jason and Kristyn." We ran up a huge tab, and Kristyn's great-grandfather, whom she'd never met, paid the bill. I don't remember too many times that both our families came together for a celebration like this. It was a memory we'll always cherish.

Since high school, we always talked about having three kids, but so far we've only had two. Kristyn gave birth to Jason Jr. eight weeks early, so we couldn't bring him home for a couple of weeks. Next came a girl, Bella, several years later. From the day JJ, as we call him, was born, I committed myself to bring him up in a home centered on love. Love for God, foremost, him seeing me loving Kristyn, and him knowing I love him.

I've seen that modeled by Kristyn's father, Randy, many times. Both as a father and a husband to his wife, Susan, whom I lovingly call Mamasita. Kristyn and I have tried to find the best attributes in our parents as well as in other couples and model them as much as we can. They're not perfect, and we're certainly not.

We know that an active church life can keep us on track. We became involved in Woodlands Church just north of Houston early in our marriage, and we considered the many opportunities to serve.

God gave me a burden for the homeless. I'm thankful that I always managed to find a friend willing to let me sleep with a roof over my head, but others are not so fortunate.

We delivered meals to them throughout the year, and when Thanksgiving came around, I wanted to smoke a bunch of turkeys for our less fortunate friends benefiting from the ministry. To do so, I needed time off and didn't have any vacation days left. Randy and Mamasita had begun attending Woodlands with us. I was nervous to ask for time off, but Randy agreed, knowing the importance of that ministry. More importantly, I think he witnessed the work God was doing in my life by serving in that way.

Nothing is more important than my faith in God. Kristyn and I both believe that we're called to love God more than we love one another. When a devout Jewish leader asked Jesus what the greatest commandment was, Jesus answered, "The most important is, 'Hear, O Israel: The Lord our God, the Lord is one. And you shall love the Lord your God with all your heart and with all your soul and with all your mind and with all your strength'" (Mark 12:29-30). After that, Jesus said, is loving our neighbor. My wife and kids would certainly seem to rank higher than my neighbor. However, the basic meaning is clear, that loving God is greater than loving another human. I know that loving God with a blazing, white-hot devotion, above all other humans, will be a greater gift to Kristyn and my kids than anything else I could give them. I haven't always done that, of course, but I know I need to. It's something I work on every day.

I say all that to close with this. The second most important thing in my story, after God, is Kristyn. She is the linchpin that holds everything together. There is no me without her. She's been there every step of the way. She could have given up on me any number of times. She never did. She loves her Heavenly Father, and she loves me. What a precious gift God gave me. I star her!

***

From Kristyn:

Once I began to mature, I never looked for Prince Charming or the perfect jock boyfriend. Flowers are nice, but I wanted depth. Someone that didn't mind sharing the deep things in life. Someone that loved long conversations. I didn't care if they were wounded. In fact, I sought someone that had traveled a hard road and lived to tell about it. My father had it tough growing up and wanted me to find someone that could build me up, not tear me down.

My second time meeting Jason seemed like the first since I didn't recognize him.

I asked my friend, "Who's that guy. He's hot!"

"You've met him before," she said.

"Remember that day on the walking path? He and Will were running from the police or something."

Then it dawned on me. I did remember him. A guy had just broken up with me, and I certainly wasn't looking for a relationship. We connected so quickly it actually concerned me. I didn't know if I was ready for another relationship but soon realized that we were destined for one another. He wrote me letters constantly and treated me with so much respect. We grew our relationship on an emotional level rather than a physical one. I'd never met anyone that I could talk to about everything.

At first, he talked a lot about his enlistment in the military. It's not that he was obsessed with it but, rather, committed. I thought this would be a summer romance, and then I'd never see him again. I soon realized that wouldn't be the case. Not by a long shot. He asked me to have dinner at his house to meet his parents. I'm a shy person, so I worried they'd overwhelm me. I knew his relationship with his father had been tumultuous. That first night was awkward, but they warmed up to me. His sister would soon enter high school, so we became great friends.

My friends didn't care for our relationship. They focused more on social status at school or things I had no interest in. I wanted out of that group and went to night school so I could graduate early. I only wanted to be with Jason. We became inseparable.

During the period where my father didn't want us to see one another, we would meet at the picturesque Oyster Creek Park in Sugar Land. We would usually meet there at night when there were few to no people. We'd lay on a blanket, have picnics, and talk next to this rose bush that we designated as our rose bush. One night we lay there looking up at the stars together and talked about how much we loved each other. We had deep discussions about our feelings, which seemed to be so much deeper than love.

"I star you," Jason said as we looked up at the stars.

That became our thing to say instead of I love you. It was sort of code but also our special little thing and something we say to this day. Whenever we're going through a rough patch, we drive to Oyster

Creek Park and sit in our spot. Sadly, the rose bush is gone, but the stars are still there. It reminds us of how we started.

When he popped the question, he certainly surprised me with the elaborate details, but I knew it was coming eventually. I never doubted that I'd say yes.

We planned a big wedding in Hawaii for the next year when many of the SERVPRO clan would be there for a convention. However, a little surprise derailed our wedding plans.

One day, Jason said, "I think you're pregnant?"

"No way," I said.

"You should get a pregnancy test. I know you are."

I thought he was full of it. I bought one just to prove him wrong. Well, he was right.

My dad had kept bugging Jason about when he'd give him a grandson or granddaughter. I don't think he meant that soon, but when we took him to lunch and told him, he was ecstatic. He screamed, "Woohoo!" in the restaurant. We took Jason's parents to a Chinese restaurant to tell them. Jason opened a fortune cookie and said, "You will have a small surprise by the end of the year." He was making that up, of course. His parents were thrilled as well.

I didn't want either the baby, or I, to not have the last name Hollen. I also didn't want to be seven or eight months pregnant walking down the aisle. So, we rushed to have the wedding just six weeks later. As my dad gave me away, a tear rolled down Jason's cheek. He's a crier, and I love that about him. He's never been afraid to be vulnerable or show his emotions around me. We honeymooned in Playa del Carmen,

Mexico, where we did some deep-sea fishing and cave dwelling, and rested our feet on white, sandy beaches.

Just before JJ came, I remembered so much my father had taught me about faith. He would read the Bible to me as a little girl and tell me how important it was to have a relationship with Jesus.

"You have a new soul coming into the world. You get to mold him," my father said, likely thinking about Jason's past and the difficulties he had as a child. "You get to train your child to love Christ."

Following my father's advice, we've tried to do just that. I'm so proud of those times when, after JJ learned to write, he'd write out verses from the Bible or craft a little note to Jason that was saturated with Jesus.

I would love to say that our marriage "hasn't always been easy." That seems too simplistic. I think any husband or wife could say that. Ours has been incredibly difficult at times. But our love for God and love for one another has carried us through the darkest of times. Ours is truly a love story. I'm so thankful that God brought me Jason and now JJ and little Bella. They're everything to me.

Chapter 6:
Preparing to Launch

After the Japanese attack on Pearl Harbor, radio broadcasts spread the news across the nation. Young men asked the question, "Where do I sign up?" They all knew a national response required military action. Each one had to consider how they'd serve their patriotic duty in defense of their nation.

A full year after I had left the detention center, I sat with Kristyn watching TV on the first anniversary of 9/11. I'd never actually seen the footage of planes slamming into the World Trade Center towers. I'd certainly heard about the horror of that day but to see the towers fall, the people running and covered in ash, made me realize the terror of that day. Anger welled up in me. It's the feeling I assumed all those that joined up after Pearl Harbor felt. I wanted to do something, right then and there. I wanted to defend my country. So many men and women of my generation have answered the call to serve in the War on Terror just as those that responded in 1941.

I already had a leaning toward military service. During my freshman year of high school, I joined the ROTC. My buddy Chris had benefited from it and encouraged me to give it a try. I embraced the discipline, knowing I needed that structure in my life. Captain Heatherington led our group with zero tolerance for shenanigans. He ran a tight ship, as they say. I respected him deeply and worked hard to earn his respect. When one sees leadership, it's almost innate to want to follow. God had continued to place role models in my life. We stayed busy with extracurricular activities, such as camping, orienteering, and drill team. I loved to don that uniform once per week as they required. He wouldn't hesitate to smack us in the head with a book, to get our attention, more like a tap, a comical thing, that is. Like a football coach, he meted out punishments for our failure to accomplish tasks. This usually included physical exercise or more difficult orienteering challenges. I did well with a compass, but it frustrated me if I didn't make the best time. Their punishments and corrections weren't senseless. They had a greater end in mind.

My parents encouraged my involvement in this organization and got to know the captain as well as our other instructor, Chief Watson, another no-nonsense leader I revered. Early in the program, and prior to my confinement, they had met with me and my parents about an opportunity to attend the New Mexico Military Institute in Roswell on a full scholarship. I was ecstatic and wanted to go. It seemed like an opportunity for a fresh start away from negative influences. My dad had no interest in me doing life that far away out of his control. He told them "no" and crushed my hope at this new opportunity. Nonetheless, I stayed in ROTC both before and after my period of lock-up.

Captain Heatherington really pushed me, and I embraced it. ROTC certainly encouraged enlistment in one of the military branches, and my call toward that only grew. Beyond that, I'm confident I would have never graduated high school without them. My grades had never been an issue, but ROTC gave me the drive to achieve something more lasting. They taught me military bearing. It's a foreign concept for some, but it essentially means the inclination for following orders and working as a team. While I sorely lacked discipline in many areas of my life, it's always been my goal to live an orderly life.

With images of 9/11 in my head and a strong foundation from ROTC, I determined to join the military after graduation. After my time away in lock-up, I had gained a substantial amount of weight. A couple of friends that had joined the Marine Corps helped me workout. They'd pick me up at 5:00 AM, and we'd head to Lost Creek Park in Sugar Land, Texas, to work out and train in hand-to-hand combat. I'd shower afterward and head to school. That, in addition to lifting weights, became my regular routine, and the pounds fell off. I lost about seventy pounds in just a few months and felt ready for anything the military would throw at me.

Late in my junior year, the courts freed me from probation, and I had not been on regular medication. If there was ever going to be a time they'd let me join, this was it. I admired what Chris did in the Navy, and Captain Heatherington and Chief Watson pushed me toward joining that branch. One of our ROTC drills had us spend two weeks at sea living on a Navy ship. I hated the confined spaces. It reminded me too much of prison, so I ruled that out. All that time I spent working out with Marines made me lean toward them. However, during another ROTC trip with the Army, we saw the M1 Abrams tank up close. They even let me drive it a short distance. I drove a tank before I ever drove a car. That hooked me. I wanted to join the armory and blow stuff up. Simple as that.

For me to join, my parents had to agree since I had yet to reach my eighteenth birthday. I don't think my mother was ever comfortable with me joining, but my father signed. He knew I'd go at eighteen anyway. The Delayed Entry Program allowed high schoolers to join early and credit that time as Individual Ready Reserves. The military requires almost everyone in the service to perform a period of inactive duty after their active years. This program allowed us to give up to one year of service prior to active duty. We drilled periodically, spent time at nearby Fort Hood, and learned the lingo that we'd need in basic training. I maintained my physical readiness but hid my substance abuse. The military had zero tolerance for that. None of it stopped my partying ways.

Chris knew all about me. He knew of the partying, but he had great concerns over my tendency toward rage from my bipolar condition. My temperament, uncontrolled by medication, could spark anger in an instance. What I see as raising my voice is seen as aggressiveness by others. Chris had served in combat in Afghanistan and worried I might cause myself or my fellow soldiers harm on some faraway battlefield. He urged me to reconsider a career in the military.

I had enough credits to graduate early in 2002 and planned to ship out in January of 2003, just weeks shy of my eighteenth birthday. Two weeks before Christmas, a letter arrived from the Army stating that they had declined my enlistment over concerns about my mania. I'm pretty sure Chris made that happen, but I've never been upset with him over that. I know he loved me like a brother and only had concerns for my best interest. As hard as I had worked to prepare, it actually gave me some relief. Being head over heels in love with a girl will do that to you. Kristyn was overjoyed. Looking back now, it's hard to say what my time in the military would have produced, but I know that staying by Kristyn's side saved my life.

With this new direction, I planned to stay in high school, work part-time, and earn extra credits in preparation for college. I leaned toward earning an accounting degree. I enjoyed working with numbers and the orderliness of accounting. My father wanted me to move back in and attempted to set some boundaries and impose a curfew on me. Essentially, a "my house, my rules" ultimatum. I scoffed, but he wouldn't let me have a key. So, I had to be home by a certain time if I wanted in the house. As part of meeting these new standards, he planned to buy me a car once I earned my driver's license. I took the driving test on my eighteenth birthday and my dad handed me the keys to a 1992 Toyota Corolla.

My parents took me and Kristyn out that night to celebrate, and my father made sure I had plenty to drink. It worked, and I was drunk. I handed my keys to Kristyn, but he took them and told me to "be a man." Compared to other substance abuse, I think he placed alcohol in a different category. An acceptable one, perhaps. At that age, I picked my battles with my father. He had tried to get me to stop smoking countless times, but I never relented on that one. I had no fear of him physically, but part of me wanted to please him. I had screwed up so many times, I tried to make up for that with moments of obedience. So, I drove Kristyn to her home and then made it back to my house. Day one as a licensed driver had ended.

After high school graduation, I worked full-time at a machine shop. My father had gotten me the job through his company, at a different location than his. I didn't care for the work but appreciated the paycheck that allowed me to live in my own apartment. I worked nights and then attended Wharton County Junior College in the morning. The schedule wore me down, and I eventually stopped school after two semesters.

One of those listless nights at the machine shop, I began to move a large metal part with an overhead crane. The chain broke, and the crane hook swung down, striking me in the mouth. I'm unsure how long I was unconscious, but eventually I woke up and headed toward the bathroom mirror to survey the damage. Only two of us worked in the shop that night, and the other guy was somewhere else. My jaw and mouth had been severely cut. I felt no pain due to the shock, but I knew I needed help getting to the hospital.

Once I arrived at the hospital, the pain arrived as well. The hook had sheared several of my teeth in half, and the deep cut required over thirty stitches. I spent the next two months on disability and drank most of my meals through a straw before graduating to soft food. My mom gave me Jell-O shots to help. Someone might have cautioned her that giving alcohol to an addict on pain medication is a dangerous combination, but of course, I didn't argue. I ended up quitting that job.

I didn't care for it, and I feared another injury in that environment with the dangerous equipment.

Due to exposed nerves, it was some of the worst pain I had ever experienced. The cold weather or a cold drink exacerbated the agony. The doctor had prescribed me hydrocodone. Because it's what I always did, I had to experiment with that to see if I could get high. I tried taking several at once and hated it. I never considered abusing opioids after that.

In reality, I had been using cocaine and meth (methamphetamine) the whole time. I experienced cocaine for the first time during my freshman year of high school—it was part of my routine I shared earlier, which began with getting high Thursday or Friday, continuing on Saturday, and crashing on Sunday. Cocaine offers a quick euphoric high and a feeling of adrenaline. It made me want to do anything and everything. I'd talk constantly. In later years I'd experience paranoia while on cocaine, but in those earlier years, cocaine made me feel invincible. The high lasted thirty minutes to an hour. I never had an issue finding the drug. I had a knack for spotting the guy in the neighborhood selling, and since so many of my fellow students had the money to buy it, the sellers were eager to supply the demand.

I started meth after high school. I had always feared that drug in high school but at eighteen learned to snort or smoke it for a high lasting eight to ten hours. When given the choice, I preferred cocaine. Meth mostly kept me in a good mood but made me feel even stronger, which could lead to more aggressiveness. Neither are safe drugs, but the long-lasting meth is more disruptive to normal life. Coming down off these drugs didn't have the hangover effect of alcohol, but more allergy-like symptoms, like congestion and sniffing. In extreme situations, it gave me nosebleeds. In my thinking at the time, that was a mild trade-off. I had no rational belief in how harmful they were. I had no idea that I'd eventually burn a hole through my septum.

By the time I began working in the machine shop, I used every day. Even during the graveyard shift at work while running a honing machine that shapes finished metal pieces. I'd set the machine to run on auto for twenty minutes and then sneak out to my car for a quick hit of cocaine. I'd get home at 4:00 AM, take a shower, eat, head to school at 7:30 AM. The drugs kept me up, and then I'd drink alcohol to come back down. I thought I needed those to power me through the brutal cycle of working and attending school full-time. Some days I slept, some days I didn't.

As mentioned, I eventually gave up on college, and when I wasn't working I earned a degree in partying. Sometimes I'd wake up and find people in my apartment I didn't even know. Friends of friends, I assumed. The place looked like we robbed a gaming store with the latest console of the day. Video games stacked everywhere. Remnants of drugs. Empty bottles and cans of alcohol. Every day. A den of iniquity.

On the day of the accident, I had done a tremendous amount of cocaine and might have even done a little meth. I hadn't slept in days. I really don't know if the machine malfunctioned, or if all those factors contributed. Regardless, that damage to my face gave me a wakeup call to stop the drugs. I still drank. I still smoked cigarettes. I still took medication for my bipolar disorder, but the cocaine and meth had to go.

That lasted for six months before I did what I always did—returned to my old demons.

Although I loved my relationship with Kristyn and found contentment in that, I lacked any ambition for a career or any job whatsoever. This poor mental state steered me toward using drugs and alcohol to uncontrollable levels. My mother came by my apartment one day to check on me and found me in dire straits. She said I couldn't speak or walk and called an ambulance. I'm sure many of my friends and family assumed they'd one day find me unconscious. Maybe a low pulse or no pulse. Eyes half-closed. The small excerpt in some local online news source would state "Man, 19, dead after an overdose of meth, cocaine, and alcohol."

The emergency room admitted me to the hospital. I awoke confused and found IVs in my arm. I should have appreciated that she was trying to care for me, but I only resented it.

My friend Matt had come by to check on me. Completely different from me, with my lack of public service, he served the community as a police officer; he's an upstanding citizen and didn't use drugs or abuse alcohol. He's sort of like the anti-Jason. He explained what had happened and that my mom called 911. I wanted to leave and ripped the IVs from my arms. Against his better judgment, he agreed to let the hospital sign me out to his care. Rather than expressing gratitude, I went my own way after walking out of the hospital. I bought a bottle of whiskey and attempted to medicate my way. I experimented with different drugs and alcohol in some ill-advised plan to keep me sane, but it accomplished nothing but more pain and misery. I pushed away anyone trying to help. Essentially, I wanted an end to everything.

Anyone suggesting that most of these problems were self-inflicted wounds would stand on solid thinking. But another element lies underneath. Even during sober times, the mania took my mind to dangerous places. Yes, illicit drugs and alcohol exacerbated the problem, but without normal meds controlling the mania, my thoughts and actions didn't mirror anything rational. A small thing could set me off that would lead me toward a full minute of rage with no inclination to stop.

Before Kristyn and I married, we stayed with my grandparents for a long weekend camping trip. I always enjoyed my time with them. My grandmother had been the first one to teach me about God and the Scriptures. During that trip, my grandfather screamed for me. I ran up to find my grandmother clutching her chest. I held her in my arms as she faded away and died. Needless to say, that traumatic event sent me into a manic phase.

A few days later, my sister, Brandy, called Kristyn a name I didn't care for, and I reacted by throwing an empty plastic soft drink bottle at her. A harmless weapon, but the action panicked my mother and she called the police. My parents called the police many times, fearing a violent episode, but on the vast majority of occasions, professionals experienced in mental health were needed, not law enforcement.

After the event that sent me away for a year, I can understand that they feared it happening again, but most were false alarms. Sometimes, I just became upset like anyone else. I argued with people as we humans do. It's just that for me, the line between the normal emotion of anger and full-on rage was blurred.

Most of the time, my mind trended toward me harming myself, not others. Some people suggest that suicide is a selfish act. The easy way out. That might be true in some cases. Although, for me it was never about doing what was easy. I simply thought, what's the point of continuing life? The only thing I had to live for was Kristyn. I always thought of her and how, if I gave up, I'd cause her pain. I simply couldn't do that to her.

Does sin play a role in suicide? It certainly can, but suicide is not the unforgivable sin some religions teach it is. One's sinful behavior might cause their trajectory toward taking their own life. However, our society has failed to recognize how much mental illness contributes to suicide. It's difficult to put into words how much mania wreaks havoc on me. Imagine a mind constantly racing with thoughts and images popping in and out. Good thoughts, bad thoughts, crazy thoughts, and mundane thoughts. The mind won't rest. Unmedicated, sleep is near impossible. When I say that "I didn't sleep for three days," I don't mean I had a few rough nights with little sleep. I literally mean I stayed awake for sixty hours straight and then crashed for eighteen hours. There's a reason some use sleep deprivation for torture. Rationality goes out of the window. Medicated, my mind can rest. I get to sleep like a normal person. I think like a normal person. I don't consider taking my life.

I ache for those with extreme mental conditions for whom medication fails to intervene. The pain and chaos overwhelm them to a point where only one solution makes sense—suicide. They simply want the turmoil to end. They reach a point where they're done fighting.

How should we treat those with mental illness? In other words, what should our attitude toward them be? Whenever Jesus encountered someone with a mental illness, he practiced compassion. He also called out the Enemy's influence on the person. Satan and Jesus had two vastly different missions. "The thief comes only to steal and kill and destroy. I came that they may have life and have it abundantly" (John 10:10).

The book of James helps us here. "Is anyone among you suffering? Let him pray. Is anyone cheerful? Let him sing praise. Is anyone among you sick? Let him call for the elders of the church, and let them pray over him, anointing him with oil in the name of the Lord. And the prayer of faith will save the one who is sick, and the Lord will raise him up. And if he has committed sins, he will be forgiven" (James 5:13-15). In that short passage, relief and aid are offered to the sick and forgiveness to those that have sinned.

People always sin. Sometimes their sin causes their illness. Sometimes illness happens through no fault of their own. Essentially, we're not called to ignore or judge them based on how they received their illness, only to pray over them for healing. Imagine if we made that our initial treatment when encountering those with mental illness—compassion and prayer.

***

From Kristyn:

It's hard to imagine a time when we couldn't instantly access a video of almost anything on our phones. In 2002, an internet search might produce that subject one searched for, but regardless, the events of 9/11 were visible all over. It surprised me that Jason had never actually seen the footage. It fascinated me to watch his reaction on that first anniversary. As teens approaching the age of military service, we all had friends that made statements about joining the armed forces and quite a few followed through on that promise.

As Jason showed that same patriotic fervor, I had mixed emotions. I couldn't fault him for that desire, but I also thought about the danger. By this time, reports of soldiers killed in Afghanistan appeared on the news almost weekly. This was the real deal. We were at war.

We're both determined people. Some might call it stubbornness, but we have an independent streak that makes it so when we set our minds to something, we make it happen. Once he decided, he didn't do it halfway. He took his ROTC seriously, and those Marines kept him working hard to get in physical shape. I'd be lying if I said I wasn't relieved when I found out his enlistment had been canceled. By then, we were head over heels in love.

As we approached high school graduation, we didn't exactly have solid plans. I had thought we'd marry someday, but we both knew we each needed to build some sort of career. Like a lot of people our age, we dabbled in college classes while searching for the right major. I watched as Jason worked and took a few classes, but could tell he had other activities going on. I knew he drank, many times to excess, but I didn't realize he had taken a deep dive into cocaine and meth.

Someone might suggest I should have known everything that was going on. I understand that assumption, but many addicts master the hiding of their abuse. When you're close to an addict, there are certainly signs to look for, but at that age, it wasn't as if I had a lot of experience in the matter. He is a hard worker. He always has been, but I didn't realize much of his extra income went toward drug purchases. If he was high from meth or cocaine, I thought it was the alcohol or maybe a little pot. Trust me, I wish I would have known the signs to look for because I absolutely would have said something.

Now I could list many things I could have been on the lookout for then: secrecy, dropping activities, denial. In case someone reading this has a loved one with a potential addiction, I wouldn't want to steer anyone in the wrong direction just because they see one sign of addiction, though. I'd encourage them to gently approach their loved one about changes they see occurring, but know free resources exist to help you through the problem and which will ensure your anonymity.

I'd rather offer one important message for the person who's loved one is an addict, whether you're a spouse, parent, or child, know that it's not your fault! During the trial of addiction, the addict will blame anything and everyone for the reasons they drink or get high. Stress, money problems, lack of love, I could go on and on. They have to take ownership of their problem. If a spouse believes they drove their significant other to drink, or if a parent believes their son or daughter is addicted to meth because they didn't love them enough as a child, it only feeds the monster of addiction. Don't buy into that mentality.

I think it's important to help them see their problem is not unique. It's happened to many before them, but there is a way out. "Therefore let anyone who thinks that he stands take heed lest he fall. No temptation has overtaken you that is not common to man. God is faithful, and He will not let you be tempted beyond your ability, but with the temptation he will also provide the way of escape, that you may be able to endure it" (1 Corinthians 10:12-13). That verse is a great comfort to me in my own life, and that truth can offer great power to one whose sin has taken over their life.

Chapter 7:
A Final Trip Down

I reached a crossroads as a nineteen-year-old with an uncertain future.

The military wouldn't take me. I had no interest in college. I really didn't care for machine shop work. I had to do something. Society expected me, a grown man, to work and provide food, clothing, and shelter for myself and, if applicable, a family. I went back to the machine shop for two weeks, then left there for a vet clinic job, caring for animals as I had done during one of my required probation jobs. I even worked with my father in his side business making small machine parts. Since I wasn't in school, I wanted to stay busy and make extra money. But none of these seemed like great, long-term options.

Kristyn worked for her dad, Randy, in his restoration business—SERVPRO. When a family's home or a business has a disaster, large or small, a restoration company arrives to stop the damage, and then clean up, dry up, and restore that property to get the family or business owner back to normal life as soon as possible. Her father owned several Houston-area locations and had pioneered a business model that took crews and equipment where storms had ravaged entire communities. While Kristyn worked in the office, I started working with the crews in the field.

For the most part, I enjoy the work. When a storm hits, literally or figuratively, we have the opportunity to provide some calm and hope. We know what to do because we've seen that type of damage before. Whether it's a fire, a flood, or another disaster, we quickly remove or protect personal property and, in most cases, start the dryers to minimize mildew and save carpeting. Then, the construction crews repair or replace anything that needs it. We restore, pure and simple. That theme of restoration has been a strong one in my life.

Hurricane Katrina landed in August 2005, devastating the city of New Orleans. Massive flooding led to most of the deaths, with totals reaching more than 1,200. Randy had promoted me to a supervisor position, and both of us temporarily moved to Louisiana to facilitate as much restoration as possible to a group of people that had lost so much. For seven or eight months we started and completed one job after another. Once it wound down, I returned to Houston to marry my bride.

The first year of marriage can certainly challenge young couples. Add a baby three months after the wedding, and the adulting gets real, super fast. We loved it, though, and look back at it now as one of the best years of our life. I absolutely loved Kristyn and

JJ. Anytime thoughts of suicide crept in, no matter how bad things were, how far my mind raced, I knew I could never let our son grow up without a father.

There were still some really bad times. Times I literally held a gun to my head. Ever since that near-fatal day in my closet when the hanger rod broke, the idea of taking my own life remained, causing a real struggle. But, then I'd think of JJ and put the gun down. I continued my drinking and stayed on my prescribed medication but managed to avoid any illegal drugs during this period. We moved into a cozy rental home, and Kristyn kept at her studies. A busy life, but a happy one. Between the two of us, we did well enough financially to support ourselves.

The pattern of addiction reared its head again as I began another spiral downward and started abusing my medications. I knew that it would only get worse and told Kristyn I had to check into a rehab facility. The news devastated her. Imagine being a young mother, one year into marriage, and your husband lays that news on you. She knew about my addictions and had witnessed my out-of-control temper, but this would be the first time those problems would separate us. Fortunately, her father provided that calming and in-charge voice for our family. I love that Randy exhibited leadership for her. I know she is strong because she had a strong mentor.

By now, I was an old pro at these facilities, but for the first time, I entered under my own free will. I could leave if I wanted this time. The rehab's main goal was to get me on the correct medication, properly administered, as well as to provide counseling for me to stay on that course. Rather than enter reluctantly, or fighting it, I entered willfully. Kristyn visited me every night and encouraged me.

Early in our marriage, we attended church on a regular basis and involved ourselves in ministries and Bible studies. The pastor and other members who walked this road with us also visited me during that difficult time. They could see the struggles I had and offered support. They lived out what Paul told the church in Ephesus: "So then you are no longer strangers and aliens, but you are fellow citizens with the saints and members of the household of God, built on the foundation of the apostles and prophets, Christ Jesus himself being the cornerstone, in whom the whole structure, being joined together, grows into a holy temple in the Lord. In Him you also are being built together into a dwelling place for God by the Spirit" (Eph. 2:19-22). They truly made me feel like a member. I had great optimism that this would work. I left on time with a solid plan. I really wanted to fight for myself and for my family. I was restored, if you will.

I didn't have much experience with church. As I've mentioned, I didn't grow up "in the church," as some would say. I had only attended a handful of times in my youth with friends. I never seriously studied the Bible until doing so with George in juvenile detention. In essence, I didn't really know how "to do" church. I was a newbie. For example, the men's Bible study group invited me to attend a gathering at a restaurant. So, what did I do? I ordered a margarita, of course. I didn't know any better. I thought, hey, it's a social gathering. Isn't everyone drinking? Not that alcohol, in moderation, is a sin, but it turns out one doesn't normally consume alcohol at a church-related gathering. Moreover, as an alcoholic, I had no business drinking at all.

I'd sit in church and listen to sermons and sometimes wonder if the pastor was speaking directly to me. We've all had that feeling, that the pastor or speaker knows that awful thing we've done. They don't, of course, and are typically preaching based on a book of the Bible or a topic that the Holy Spirit led them to. Yet, the Spirit knows us and helps to deliver that message whether we like it or not.

Meanwhile, deep down, I knew it was wrong for me to continue drinking, but we addicts are masters at justifying our actions. In fact, my drinking at that point had gotten out of hand, forcing another stay in rehab. I wouldn't say the plan from the last rehab stay failed, but rather, I failed the plan. Kristyn, the church, and my friends continued to walk that hard road with me. Everyone had concerns for me, but I cannot imagine how difficult that was for Kristyn. She's an incredibly courageous woman and partner.

I emerged, once again, with a new attitude and plan to manage my life. I returned to work and strived to perform as hard as I could for SERVPRO. My only trouble came when my meds threw off my circadian rhythm, causing me to fall asleep at my desk. It was not an issue of laziness, because I would have gladly worked through the night if needed. These medications attempted to control the mania so I could have a normal 24-hour cycle, but they'd occasionally fail. This slight distraction didn't deter me from bigger and better things in my work life.

I enjoyed my job but began to tire of the constant travel for out-of-town storm-chasing jobs, and I had reached the highest I'd ever receive in both promotions and salary. Kristyn and I discussed other opportunities even if that meant moving from Houston. We hired a broker to look for a business such as landscaping or something I could run on my own. We found a SERVPRO that I could buy in San Antonio, but Randy hated the idea of his daughter and grandson moving away. In 2012, he offered me an incredible opportunity to buy one of his Houston SERVPRO franchises.

I jumped at the chance to take on this challenge. It was both scary and exciting at the same time. Scary in that I had to do most everything in the field, with Kristyn running the office, and neither of us receiving an automatic paycheck. My first hire, Evan, helped me manage the workload. When I wasn't selling our services, I was on a job. The long hours paid off, and we did well, doubling our business in each year of the first three years. After those first three years, I allowed myself to take a breath and relax. As I progressed from owner/operator to owner, I chose to back out of micromanaging specific jobs and stay focused on big-picture aspects of the business. I look at opportunities to grow us, while allowing managers to use their talents and expertise to make sure we perform a specific job with excellence. I love the restoration business and the knowledge that we're helping people. Sometimes employees or customers present a difficulty, but we work through it and stay focused on the task at hand—restoration.

Despite the rollercoaster of using drugs and abusing alcohol, I had periods of putting them to the side and producing quality work. I loved on my wife and son. God never departed from me no matter how much I did to drive him away. A couple of years before I bought the business, I began attending classes focused on transcendental meditation. I know that many reading this may have concerns about that practice since it has roots in Hinduism. I assure you, I never have and never would worship in that religion. Simply put, I used that practice to clear my mind of all the junk and distractions and then focus on prayer and Scripture. "But his delight is in the law of the Lord, and on his law he meditates day and night" (Psalm 1:2). That's what I wanted to do. Meditate on the things of God.

Although I had been into meditation for years, these particular classes helped me gain insight into whatever happened to me during the day by then clearly showing me solutions for any problems. I didn't want some supernatural voice but would rather have clarity in thought. Essentially, I'd begin by focusing on one word and then expand my mind (transcend) to a place that focused on joy or more solution-oriented thoughts. My goal had always been a deeper relationship with Jesus Christ. Away from booze and drugs, God showed me deep things in Scripture and gave me the confidence to trust in Him and Him alone. With the hectic life I lived during that time, that twice-per-week visit to focus on prayer and meditation slowed things down. As much as I pushed my way down that spiral, God would bring me back up.

You know how they say it gets worse before it gets better? Well, that's true here too, as an old problem was fueled by a huge influx of cash. The business did so well, I made a ton of money. The kind of money where I could spend thousands of dollars on cocaine without Kristyn noticing. In one seven- to eight-month period, I spent forty thousand dollars on cocaine. It's hard to say when it started, but sometime during the building of the business, I'd drink six margaritas at lunch and then snort cocaine in the office bathroom. My recklessness was beyond comprehension. I'd drive from one place to another in a paranoid state. Nervous that if pulled over, the amount of cocaine in my truck would send me to prison. On at least two occasions, I had accidents after blacking out. No other cars or people were involved, but the police arrived, and I somehow managed to talk my way out of each situation.

I might take a break for a few days so I could sleep, but then I'd begin the cycle over again. By 2015, my daughter, Bella, was born, and while things seemed normal on the surface, my life had headed progressively downhill. Yet, I considered myself invincible. Stronger than anyone. Kristyn, however, had more strength than I could imagine. She learned of my secret—my out-of-control cocaine use. I'd lie to her that I stopped or say I didn't have any. I had ingenious hiding spots, such as the gas cap compartment of my truck, but she'd find it. She could have justifiably said, "I'm done!" but she didn't. She fought me, but she was really fighting for our family. Don't mess with momma bear!

I have feared sharing so much of my life because there are parts so ugly, I find it disgusting. I have a greater end goal, though, so I've made a conscious decision to open the vault and share openly and honestly. So, if you're wondering how much worse it can get, allow me to add one more incomprehensible layer.

I mentioned earlier how a couple of guys preached racial hatred to me in juvenile detention. There, I witnessed a separation of the races. It formed like something out of *The Lord of the Flies*. The whites welcomed me and made me a member based on the color of my skin. I shrugged and complied. I had no foundation to disagree with the things they said. I watched each race form clicks and fight one another, and saw no one make an effort to "reach across the aisle," other than George. The facility made no effort to create or end the practice.

I don't mean to come across as ignorant or uncaring, but quite simply, as a sixteen-year-old that had grown up under influential adults that had told me the same things about race, I was ignorant about the matter and frankly didn't care. I cared much more about how I'd survive in lock-up and go home. As the years progressed, I didn't join a hate group, or post online rants about members of other races, but somewhere deep inside remained hateful thoughts that could manifest themselves under times of influence from substance abuse. That's a nuanced way of saying that I might say something really stupid when drunk.

January 27, 2018, was the night that broke me. A few weeks prior, our business had been working on a multi-million-dollar project. Several temporary employees were working for us. A couple of them, both African Americans, had made some racist and sexist comments to our future customers. We lost the project due to that. In my thinking at the time, I took their race and their racism as a reinforcement of my beliefs on the matter. Stupid, I know.

On that January night, I attended a monster truck show with friends and my family, including Kristyn and my son. I began drinking beer early and became drunk by the time we headed to the parking lot. I really don't know how it started, but I approached an innocent African American woman who was surrounded by her family. I launched into a rant complete with profanity and the N-word. The altercation became so heated, a friend of mine, Jeremy, tackled me. The police arrived, broke things up, and I proceeded to pass out.

Kristyn took me to a hotel because she didn't want me at home. I woke the next day, alone, sore, and confused. I couldn't get out of bed. I had no memory of the night before and began calling people to find out how I had arrived at this strange hotel. Few took my calls. Kristyn eventually answered and told me the things I had said. I knew better than to deny it. The level of disgust was almost too much to express. I immediately thought of my son, JJ, and wondered what he might have been thinking after witnessing his father make a fool of himself. I still can't believe he saw me do this. Jeremy came to the hotel and talked for hours with me, confirming everything Kristyn had said. I kept thinking that I had become the very thing I hate. I had been disgusted with racist people in my life, and I had just embodied their belief system. To say that this was a low point in my life would be an understatement.

No wonder Kristyn had hesitated to call me back. I had screwed up before, but this was a big one. I couldn't blame it on some manic episode. While the alcohol abuse had absolutely caused it, the racist element disturbed me. Disgusting. A thousand times, absolutely disgusting!

My father-in-law found out a few days later and told me he was ashamed of me. He said he couldn't have the same relationship with me anymore. That crushed me. But worse, Kristyn had finally had enough. She was done. She wanted me gone. The ultimate intervention. Therapists told her that I wouldn't stop my addictions and destructive actions unless my world was taken away. She told me she was taking it away.

***

From Kristyn:

I'm really proud of the business my dad built and now the one Jason and I have worked so hard to develop. It's tough when your world is turned upside down by a water heater that floods your home or when a natural disaster seemingly comes right through your living room. Not only is it the family business, but the analogy of restoration in Jason's life is fitting.

When we were newlyweds, I had no doubts about the man I married. I knew we both had baggage. Of course, Jason's baggage might have been a few suitcases more than the average person's. Our love for one another had only increased from the time we had met. That first few months of marriage had some of the happiest moments, and we were overjoyed when little baby JJ entered the picture.

It didn't take long for Jason's demons to attack our marriage and family. I didn't realize he had been abusing his bipolar disorder medications to get high from them. That also meant they weren't working as intended, and his mania took him to terrible places. His mind raced and those suicidal thoughts crept back in. I was so scared but his willingness to attend rehab seemed like the best solution.

We attended a great church whose members couldn't have been more supportive. Jason and I were blessed that we always seemed to have another believer ready to walk the hard road with us. Sometimes it's family, a friend, or a church member. That's true fellowship.

As we endured these rehab stays and struggled to get a new business off the ground, I remained optimistic that we could put that old life behind us. I desperately wanted a normal life, a normal marriage, and a normal family. Some think normal is boring, but I'll take it any day. Although I had to confront Jason many times over his addiction, and many times he tried to spin his way out of it, he did seem sincere that he wanted to quit. He loved me and loved JJ deeply. I think we gave him something to fight for. I could tell he had a war raging within him with family and business pulling him one way and his addictions pulling him the other way.

It exhausted me to find yet another stash of his drugs or wonder how he had made it safely home.

When he was drunk in front of our family or friends, it embarrassed me. Some people see photos of someone in an alley, strung out on drugs, and wonder how they got there. I didn't have to wonder. I could easily envision Jason there, or in prison. Because we did financially well, so many of those problems were hidden. He could easily afford the expensive drugs, but I could tell something was wrong when tens of thousands of dollars went missing. I had reached a breaking point. I had to do something. I demanded restoration.

Chapter 8:
True Restoration

Although Kristyn told me what had happened, and I believed her, I called friends to ask how bad my actions actually were. Few took my calls. My friend Jeremy came by and revealed all the sordid details of what I had said and done the previous night. Still somewhat drunk, I couldn't believe it. I wouldn't believe it. But it was true. Every ugly detail. No wonder Kristyn had hesitated to call me back. I had screwed up before, but this was a big one. I can't blame it on some manic episode. The alcohol abuse absolutely caused it. The racist element greatly disturbed me. That certainly had no normal place in my life. Disgusting. A thousand times, absolutely disgusting! I tried calling Kristyn over and over the next couple of days to apologize and smooth things over.

Finally, she answered. "You screwed up for the last time."

I apologized profusely, but my words fell on deaf ears. She'd heard it all before. There was no pleading or begging this time.

In no uncertain terms, I wasn't welcome home until I got help. Real help. Not simply another rehab stay. For me to successfully endure those ten to fourteen days required for rehab was low-hanging fruit. I was a master at that. I contemplated this for the next several days in that lonely hotel room. My hip killed me, and I found out later that my friend had fractured it when he tackled me. I drove to an urgent care, but they couldn't do anything for the injury. They told me to stay off it so it could heal on its own. That, of course, was the least of my worries.

I thought about my business. How could I waltz into work as if nothing happened? I could imagine the look on my employees' faces once word got out. I couldn't go back, not yet, anyway. Kristyn had told them not to talk to me. I asked my parents if I could stay with them, but they said "No." I was persona non grata. Stuck in that hotel for over seven days.

My father-in-law echoed everything Kristyn said, "You're not welcome back home."

His words magnified my dilemma ten times over. Unwelcome in my own home. Unwelcome at my own company. No wife. No son. No baby daughter. Addiction took my world away. I had reached a crossroads. The culmination of a wrecked life consumed with addiction.

I can't think of a more apt passage of Scripture to describe my life at that point than this:

For I do not understand my own actions. For I do not do what I want, but I do the very thing I hate. Now if I do what I do not want, I agree with the law, that it is good. So now it is no longer I who do it, but sin that dwells within me. For I know that nothing good dwells in me, that is, in my flesh. For I have the desire to do what is right, but not the ability to carry it out. For I do not do the good I want, but the evil I do not want is what I keep on doing. Now if I do what I do not want, it is no longer I who do it, but sin that dwells within me.

So I find it to be a law that when I want to do right, evil lies close at hand. For I delight in the law of God, in my inner being, but I see in my members another law waging war against the law of my mind and making me captive to the law of sin that dwells in my members. Wretched man that I am! Who will deliver me from this body of death? (Romans 7:15-24).

Wretched! What an awful, yet perfect word. I certainly felt wretched. Many fine theologians have written commentaries on this passage, and we can learn much from them. But let me explain it as an addict, as I see it. You'd think I could easily say that I understood why I did those things. To get high or drunk. I liked both. Many times, I planned my day around it. But I knew it was wrong when I did it. I knew I could lose my family over my actions. I knew I could go to prison, hurt someone on the road, or overdose and die. Because of this, I know it was the sin that dwelt within me.

If we're honest, and we believe in God's Word, we know that nothing good dwells in us. We're born with an inclination to sin. Romans 3:23 clearly states that "all have sinned and fall short of the glory of God." Most of us have a moral compass. We want to do the right thing, but our compass sometimes points the wrong way—toward sin. We can blame it on our sinful nature, but that doesn't excuse us. We don't use God's forgiveness as a license to sin.

So, every time we weigh that moral dilemma, like the proverbial devil on one shoulder telling lies and an angel on the other whispering encouragement, we have a war waging in our mind and body. It doesn't seem fair, does it? It's there, though. We're all born this way. Wretched. It's why we're separated from God. Who can deliver us from this spiritual death? Who can help us? I never needed help more than I did at that lowest point in my life.

For goodness' sake, I owned a restoration company. How could I not see that my figurative home lay in ruins from disaster? However, it wasn't a total loss. No bulldozers needed to come. I needed restoration. When a home is damaged, especially by water, we pull up carpet, remove soaked padding, and tear out drywall. It seems as though we're doing more damage, but we have to expose every bit of moisture to prevent mold. We then bring in dryers for that same reason, and they sometimes run for days. Finally, construction crews rebuild walls, install carpet, and paint to make the home better than it was before the damage. I probably seemed like a total loss, but maybe I could be restored. I needed things exposed and dried out, a rebuild, and a fresh coat of paint.

Everyone kept telling me to go back to rehab. I don't blame them. That seemed logical. However, I knew that I'd never change unless I truly wanted to change. I had to want it more than anything. That passage from Romans 7 has one more verse, which ends the chapter: "Thanks be to God through Jesus Christ our Lord! So then, I myself serve the law of God with my mind, but with my flesh I serve the law of sin" (Romans 7:25).

Only one person could save me. Jesus Christ.

I love music, so I think about so many musicians who seem to "have it all" but succumb to drug overdose or suicide. It's almost cliché for them. Korn guitarist Brian "Head" Welch, a recovering addict, authored a book called *Save Me from Myself: How I Found God, Quit Korn, Kicked Drugs, and Lived to Tell My Story*. What a perfect title. I'll give you the spoiler. God saved Brian from himself. God helped him kick drugs and allowed him to survive to tell his story. That's true restoration. I'm thankful he wasn't one of those musicians who lost the battle of addiction. I didn't want to be a statistic either. I needed God more than ever and cried out for Him to help me.

I don't know that I can remember the exact moment. It happened over a few days sitting in that hotel room, but God gave me a miracle. I don't use that word lightly. I believe God did a miraculous work in my life. I lost all desire for alcohol and drugs. Cold turkey. It wasn't that I needed to avoid them so I wouldn't get caught or so I could pretend I was clean and sober for a few weeks to fool Kristyn. I'm saying that from that moment on, I didn't want a drop of alcohol and had no desire to get high. Poof! Gone.

I had wanted to quit my substance abuse a hundred times, but once I had numerous witnesses tell me what I had done on that awful night, and once I realized that I would lose my family and my business, I truly wanted to quit.

No, it shouldn't have taken that event for me to get sober. I wish my first ever stay in a psychiatric hospital had done the trick. I left a path of destruction for nearly twenty years with countless other regretful events that should have forced me to take a stand. Yet, that's what began my sobriety. Next came the hard part—convincing Kristyn. I can say that tongue in cheek, now, but it was serious business then. Just imagine how many times she heard me say, "This is the last time, I promise."

I had connected with my sponsor, Harold, a couple of years before at the Houston Center for Christian Counseling. He quit drinking in the 1970s and had over thirty-five years of sobriety. I reached out to him with one question. "How do I get my life back?"

He's an incredibly sweet man. With no judgment, he told me to attend as many AA (Alcoholics Anonymous) meetings as possible. I immediately followed that advice and initially attended three per day. We later met in person, and I asked him to help me clean out my car. He found several bottles of tequila and vodka, took them, and poured them out. I wanted to make sure I rid myself of every stash I could remember. He gave me a hug and assured me that he'd stand by me in this hour of trial.

I returned home under Kristyn's watchful eye. She adopted a wait-and-see attitude and had me sleep in separate quarters. I told everyone that I'd head back to rehab, but I decided on a more realistic treatment goal: attending thirty AA meetings in thirty days. I prayed every morning for God to give me the strength to stave off temptation. I'd simply take it one day at a time.

On one of my first nights back home under "family probation," our families met at a restaurant for my birthday. It was the first time I'd seen Kristyn's father since that terrible night. To say dinner was awkward would be an understatement. I felt everyone looking at me, making judgments, most of them justified, felt Kristyn and her dad looking at me and likely thinking, There's Jason, pretending to be on the road to sobriety. Probably going to fail again.

I don't blame them if that's what they thought.

My parents probably thought, There's Jason, pretending to be on the road to sobriety. What a silly idea. He's a drunk, so what?

I don't know that, but I'm not sure they believe sobriety is a viable option for some people. Overall, everyone seemed careful around me, as if unsure what to say. After all, what do you say to someone who screws up in such a monumental way?

Slowly, those around me, especially Kristyn, could see that I had changed. Had I drunk alcohol or used drugs, she would have known. But she could see the change in other areas. I had no desire to eat out, especially Tex-Mex. I had loved those restaurants for the food but even more so for the margaritas. As I reintegrated into normal work life, I ordered food in. I quit using cough medicine and mouthwash because I didn't want to come within an inch of the alcohol in those products. I realize that sounds extreme, but I did what it took for successful sobriety.

I experimented with Antabuse, a drug that causes unpleasant side effects, headaches, impotence, sore tongue, and others, when alcohol enters the body. On one occasion, several of the side effects kicked in. I didn't understand because I hadn't drunk alcohol. I later learned that my hair gel had alcohol in it and had absorbed through my skin. So, I stopped the Antabuse. I felt I had been doing really well at avoiding even a hint of alcohol without its intervention.

I'll issue a public service announcement here for those who might not know or who need a reminder: Quitting certain drugs and alcohol cold turkey can produce unpleasant and sometimes dangerous side effects. Anyone making the positive step toward sobriety should do so under the care of a physician, which usually means joining a detox program. Please don't ever let that part of quitting scare you because there are safe and tolerable ways to come off alcohol and drugs. I didn't do that and somehow escaped all those withdrawal issues. I almost feel guilty that I didn't have to suffer through that. Lucky, I suppose.

My son understood to some extent that I had a problem, and he certainly had seen some of the things I had done. We have those talks little by little and may need to do that for some time. He'll read this book one day and know it all. I only hope he sees the man I am today and not that fool who let substances take over his life. In the first weeks after I returned home, my father-in-law, Randy, and I had a few conversations. He began to see the change as well and generously counseled me with encouragement to use the opportunity to grow from my mistakes.

Admittedly, most stories like this speak of a successful stint in a rehab facility. That works for many, and as I stated before, I had been there and done that. I applaud the work of those that serve in rehab and those that successfully emerge from it. However, that isn't my story. I give God all the credit for the work he did in my life and the way He did it. By making Kristyn the strongest voice in pushing me toward sobriety and being my partner in the bad times. God also used and continues to use AA in my life in a monumental way.

Alcoholics Anonymous is responsible for helping millions overcome their addiction to alcohol and stay on the path of sobriety. It's pretty incredible for an organization that has no mandatory service fees and only requires members to have a willingness to take a step toward sobriety. In 1935, two alcoholics met one another in Akron, Ohio, via The Oxford Group, a Christian organization focused on helping people through their personal problems. The two men, known as Bill W. and Dr. Bob, began meeting when Dr. Bob had trouble staying sober. Bill W. had stopped drinking but had yet to see others make the same commitment. Through their mutual encouragement, they both maintained successful sobriety. The key lay in a form of group therapy, led by laypersons rather than an individual struggling through a medical program on their own. They felt anonymity an important component, so members don't reveal last names, and hence the "Anonymous" in the name.

The two worked with one alcoholic after another, helping them achieve sobriety with regular meetings in homes. A second group formed in New York and a third in Cleveland, Ohio. Through their initial work, they went on to found Alcoholics Anonymous and that developing group helped over 100,000 people by 1951. To date, over two million people regularly meet in a hundred thousand groups in nearly every country in the world. In most of the United States, one can easily find a meeting location near them.

Bill W. and Dr. Bob developed a set of principles foundational in fighting addiction. Known as The Twelve Steps, they've remained the method that most recovering alcoholics have used to win their addiction battle. The steps are also used in almost all forms of addiction. Here they are. We:

1. Admitted we were powerless over alcohol—that our lives had become unmanageable

2. Came to believe that a Power greater than ourselves could restore us to sanity

3. Made a decision to turn our will and our lives over to the care of God as we understood Him

4. Made a searching and fearless moral inventory of ourselves

5. Admitted to God, to ourselves and to another human being the exact nature of our wrongs

6. Were entirely ready to have God remove all these defects of character

7. Humbly asked Him to remove our shortcomings

8. Made a list of all persons we had harmed, and became willing to make amends to them all

9. Made direct amends to such people wherever possible, except when to do so would injure them or others

10. Continued to take personal inventory and when we were wrong promptly admitted it
11. Sought through prayer and meditation to improve our conscious contact with God as we understood Him, praying only for knowledge of His will for us and the power to carry that out
12. Having had a spiritual awakening as the result of these steps, we tried to carry this message to alcoholics and to practice these principles in all our affairs

If you've never been to a meeting, you've likely seen one in a movie or TV show. A group of adults exchange pleasantries, pour themselves a cup of coffee in a small, white Styrofoam cup, and take their seat in a circle or in chairs facing a podium.

A leader urges a person to start and that person says, "I'm Jason, and I'm an alcoholic."

The group says, "Hi, Jason!"

What follows is their struggle or success since the last meeting or maybe what they fear coming up. Others in the group might offer some encouragement. That first bit, stating one's first name followed by the admission that they're an alcoholic, is a vital step in acknowledging their problem.

A meeting can certainly scare a first-timer, but there's no requirement to speak or admit everything you've ever done wrong in your life. Simply attending is a great first step. The power of AA is in the testimonies of those that have experienced the same struggles. They talk about what led to their abuse of alcohol, how they overcame that, and their continued challenges. When an alcoholic involved with AA says, "I need a meeting," they mean they need their friends to help them or need that encouragement from testimony.

I first attended AA as a teen and still attend today. Since my sobriety, the meetings mean more to me than they ever have. I recently heard from one AA member that received a DWI, got bonded out, drank again, and killed a family in a car accident. He went to prison for a time and reached fifteen years of sobriety. That story is a constant reminder of why I need to maintain my sobriety. That easily could have been me.

Most AA meetings meet in a strip center or church and are self-funded by member donations. Newcomers typically meet a person there that agrees to sponsor them. The sponsor is another alcoholic that is willing to share their phone number and help guide the newbie through the twelve steps. Like Bill W. and Dr. Bob discovered, being a sponsor helps one maintain their own sobriety. As you can see, AA meetings are meant to provide a lower barrier to entry as well as a zero to low-cost option to recovery compared with a commitment to a facility.

I realize there are those that don't think AA works. They question studies of the percentage of success through AA. They might suggest another recovery program is better. They're missing the point. Recovery is the goal. AA has worked and works for many. It may not work for some, and other programs work better for certain people. I'd urge anyone to use the program that seems to work best for them, or a combination of AA and something else. I can only boast of how AA has worked for me and many others. The twelve steps have also worked for many other addictions, such as drugs, sex, overeating, and gambling.

As I woke on January 28, 2018, the morning after that fateful night, I didn't even know I'd never drink or do cocaine again. Over the next several weeks, I headed back to church, ate normal meals, and felt so much better from a health perspective. I didn't really experience a personality change or weight gain. Aside from the supervised medication for bipolar disorder, I put normal things in my body. Overall, I slept well and woke each morning focused on family or work activities. It sounds cliché, but the air seemed cleaner and food tasted better. Friends commented on how proud they were of me. In addition to AA, I met with my sponsor or spoke to them via video on a weekly basis.

Sobriety gave me a whole new world to live in. I became amazed at how much I accomplished in the first hour of the day when I wasn't hungover and could think clearly. Throughout the day, I had so much more awareness, control, concentration, and stamina. Rather than scheming how to snort cocaine or create an excuse to get drunk, I made the most of every single moment of every day. Not every vice is gone, and I don't claim to be perfect. I've smoked cigarettes since I was twelve, and it still calms me, but I am working with my doctor to quit that.

After all those stints in rehab, I'd walk out pretending to be on the road to sobriety. I either fooled others or myself. By February of 2018, I knew this was different. The miracle had actually happened. On a short road trip with Kristyn, I told her I had a greater calling in life. I wanted to speak in public to any audience that would listen and where I could make a difference. I thought that speaking to youth in juvenile detention and telling them that they didn't have to make the same mistakes as I had would have some real impact. The ministry was born at that point.

After more than ten weeks without drinking or drugs, and no desire for either, I felt recovery and restoration. I looked at Kristyn and my kids with a deep, sincere love. My business thrived. My new normal.

***

From Kristyn:

Shocking! I don't know of any other way to describe that night from hell. I heard things come out of Jason's mouth I'd never heard before. I was embarrassed, appalled, and furious, all at the same time. I didn't even want to look at him. I certainly didn't want him home or anywhere near me and the children. I thought it best to have him stay in a hotel while I had time to think. For almost sixteen years of our relationship, I had seen him fall down and get back up. I'd seen him rage and then quickly calm. I'd seen him high and dysfunctional one day but then sober and working his tail off the next. Highs and lows. It had to end. I drew my line in the sand.

I watched my phone ring over and over as he called. I didn't answer or respond to any texts. My goal wasn't to make him suffer, but I honestly had nothing to say. I didn't want to listen to the pleading for forgiveness or empty promises of change. I finally relented but stopped him from the excuse-making. I told him that he had made a fool out of himself and our family. I told him that he scared everyone around him. I told him that he could choose. Drugs and alcohol or his family. That simple. There'd be no more short stay in rehab and "let's see how it goes."

I wanted to see change before he came home and rejoined the family. I had an ally in my father. I knew that Jason deeply respected him, so any reinforcement my father provided would matter to Jason.

After several days, he laid out his plan for sobriety. It all seemed too quick. Too convenient. However, there was one major difference. Jason didn't have the attitude that he needed a treatment facility to help him quit or that he needed some period of time.

He declared, "I'm done!"

That's bold, I thought.

I respected his sponsor, Harold, and knew that he was working with him closely. Jason attended several AA meetings a day. I didn't believe in the whole quitting cold turkey thing, but it really seemed to happen that way. One day he was a drunk and then he wasn't. One day he used drugs, and then he didn't. I can't recall an exact moment that I believed it, but each day gave me more and more confidence until I realized my husband was truly sober. Praise the Lord!

Indeed, "Blessed be the Lord! For he has heard the voice of my pleas for mercy. The Lord is my strength and my shield; in him my heart trusts, and I am helped; my heart exults, and with my song I give thanks to him" (Psalm 28:6-7).

I couldn't believe God had performed that miracle for us. I got my husband back. My children got their father back. There were no stashes for me to find, no bottles of alcohol in his truck, and no money hidden for drugs. He thought clearly and could focus on us and the business. With this new sobriety came a desire to correctly use his bipolar medications. He didn't want the high from them anymore; he only wanted the control they gave, so his mind could stop racing and he could sleep a normal eight hours like everyone else.

I realized others would think he was fooling everyone and that I was naive. I didn't blame them—most of them would need more time to believe it.

However, it angered me when some mocked his new sobriety. How could they allow their cynicism to sabotage his sobriety? All I could do was trust that God would sustain Jason as I watched people offer him alcohol only to have Jason say, "No, thanks." That may not sound like much to some, but it meant everything to me.

When Jason first mentioned the idea of a ministry, I knew we had to do it. How could we not? After this miracle, we wanted to shout it from the rooftops. As passionate as Jason is about speaking to and encouraging young people struggling with addictions, I too want to put my arm around that young spouse or parent who's married to an addict and tell them there is hope. I can't promise them the same miracle, but I can promise them that God knows their hurt and has a plan for them. Their plan may not look like ours, but His will for them is perfect. It's easier on this side of sobriety to see that. I get it. I only encourage anyone to stay the course. To put their trust in Our Savior and watch Him work.

Chapter 9:
The Dreaded "C" Word

I like April Fool's Day as much as the next person, but in 2018, that day ended up being no laughing matter. That year, it also happened to fall on Easter Sunday—a day of celebration for Christians around the world. It's not uncommon for parents to work up a sweat hiding Easter eggs in Houston at that time of year, but the temperature only reached eighty-one degrees that day, making it a relatively cool Easter. We planned a visit with Kristyn's family in The Woodlands, an upscale community north of Houston. Our kids loved that we stayed in our RV, almost as if we were camping. Internally, I celebrated three months of sobriety and having control over my medication.

I'll warn you now that my story forces me to share things not normally discussed in public, and I certainly don't intend for them to seem untoward. A couple of weeks prior to Easter, I noticed abnormal, meager bowel movements followed by constipation. Medically speaking, we all "go" about the same time once per day, but I had no such luck with the daily constitutional.

By Easter, speaking frankly, I was backed up in a major way. I made a run to the drug store, searching for that magic elixir—a laxative. The family gathered for dinner, but I excused myself as the pain took away any appetite I had. Fear set in. I'd done plenty to my body in the past and knew how to treat a number of ailments, but this was new territory.

Kristyn wanted to take me to the hospital, but a little bit of denial mixed with a sleeping pill knocked me out for the night. The next morning remains somewhat of a blur as Kristyn rushed me to the hospital while the kids stayed with her dad. What I do remember is that I couldn't have my normal morning cigarette due to the abdominal pain. I remember every excruciating moment of that torment.

When someone describes an affliction, the words can seem inadequate. We've all had a splitting headache, stubbed a toe, or cut a finger, but those don't near the level I'm describing. Still, I'll try to describe this all-consuming pain. I couldn't think of anything else but a sharp, twisting wretchedness. I doubled over, rocked back, and otherwise squirmed in my car seat, trying to find a hint of relief. I lacked peripheral vision and could only see glimpses of the surrounding landscape. My mind and my heart begged for God to offer relief. Kristyn drove intently while glancing at me and wondering what lay next.

The emergency room presented an eternal wait time. I only wanted to sleep my way through the episode and pretend it wasn't happening. A nurse checked my vitals for intake. The pain had caused my blood pressure to spike, so they immediately took me back to a treatment room. A flurry of medical personnel came in and out. They poked and prodded while asking questions I couldn't answer.

At first, they thought diverticulitis was causing the problem. They administered enemas to flush me out to no avail. Doctors ordered CT scans and X-rays. I remained groggy and confused. A nurse told me that they had me on propofol.

"Isn't that what killed Michael Jackson?" I joked.

The joking didn't last long. My doctor arrived with the test results, and his grim demeanor spoke volumes. It's the first time I heard someone say it. The last thing I wanted to hear.

The doctor crossed his arms. "You may have cancer."

And there it was. The dreaded "C" word. I had some suspicions over what may have been causing the pain. I had spent hours on the internet speculating over this or that diagnosis. Cancer certainly seemed a possibility. But everyone with an odd pain or strange spot on their skin thinks it might be cancer.

I had laughed at the *Seinfeld* episode where George Costanza points to a little white mark on his face. "Never seen that before," his doctor says. "We better get a biopsy."

George, in his typical paranoid tone: "Is it cancer?"

The halfhearted doctor replies, "Well, I don't know what it is."

Poor George. And now that's how I felt. The second the doctor uttered "cancer," the questions burst forth.

"What kind?"

"How bad is it?"

"Can you fix me?"

"Am I going to die?"

That last one brought tears. Not crocodile tears, but those of anguish. I didn't want to die. More importantly, I didn't want Kristyn to be left alone. I didn't want my kids to grow up without a father. I wanted this fixed. Immediately!

Of course, the doctor couldn't answer all those questions. It's rare for medical professionals to be able to offer an accurate diagnosis until a lab analyzes the clump of cells (which have no business being there in the first place).

The mass on my colon required emergency surgery. That's the reason I was so backed up. The cause of the intense pain. So, on the day after Easter Sunday, medical staff wheeled me into an operating room. I can only describe my last conscious thoughts before the operation as those of utter defeat. The drugs. The alcohol. Prison. All of it. I thought I had my problems whipped. Now my future lay in the hands of a man with a scalpel.

What should have been a two- to three-hour surgery lasted eight hours. My doctor arrived in the recovery room and told me he had successfully removed a tumor from my colon. A tumor isn't necessarily cancerous. I knew that a benign tumor meant something much different than a malignant one. Regardless, the surgery successfully removed the dubious mass. But, how much was left? It's not as if the doctor could lay out my five-foot colon, open it wide, and inspect every inch for cancerous growth. He removed all of the invading mass he could find and hoped that any potential cancer had been eradicated.

The doctor sent the tumor to pathology and remarked that he'd have the results in two weeks. Two long, agonizing weeks. That seemed like an eternity. The news penetrated my soul. Now lucid, I focused on everything he said. How could I sleep a wink, or even function, while waiting for news on that test result? If malignant, it meant I might have more in my system, and agonizing rounds of drastic cancer treatments with no certainty of their success.

Something else had changed in my body. Through a procedure called an ostomy, a gaping hole had been formed in my stomach. The doctor connected the hole to my colon, so I had a colostomy. Kristyn told me I may have to use a colostomy bag. As in, for the rest of my life. Had the surgery been delayed any longer, my colon could have erupted and gone septic. When a body has waste, it must go, yet my body had trapped it inside. Due to the tumor, my colon could no longer function normally, so a colostomy bag would become my new normal.

Friends came and went over the next few days. They all wanted to say, "Don't worry. I'm sure it's not cancer." But they couldn't know. I didn't know. The doctor didn't know. But those who visited still boosted my confidence. I'm truly thankful for their encouraging words while an air of uncertainty hung over my head. The post-surgery pain throbbed. I wanted to go home. I wanted freedom from the hurt. I wanted it to all go away.

After four days in the hospital, I prepared to go home but didn't want to go home groggy, and irritable. The medicine, out of sync, gave me a hungover feeling. I'd love to tell you that I had the greatest medical care known to man, but some of the staff seemed inept at even simple things like proper administration of medicine. Ironically, all the years of drug abuse gave me a highly disciplined awareness of what I put in my body. I know that if I take medication too early or too late, other problems will follow.

The doctor wanted me to stay longer, but I'd had enough. I told him, "You're sending me home today." Although I knew going home meant days of waiting and racking my brain with thoughts of test results, I needed to get out of that hospital. I went home and combed the internet for everything I could find on cancer. I also joined an online cancer group. Much of what I read tried to explain the physical and mental effects of cancer. That's not an easy task. How does one explain how cancer feels?

I turned to prayer. I thought about all I had done. Would God forgive me? Should he forgive me? I had haunting visions of my wife and kids experiencing life without me. I didn't know if one of my many sins had caused the tumor. If one too many drinks or one too many snorts of cocaine had. Who can remember every sin they've committed? Did I bring this on myself, or was the man upstairs trying to get my attention? Regardless, he had my attention. I asked God to forgive me anyway. I needed healing. I needed forgiveness. I had done all this before, but I don't think I ever truly meant it. I had told myself a million times that I needed to change, but this time, I knew I had to fully surrender.

This became the most important moment of my life. I told God that if this truly was cancer, then I was ready for a fight. I made peace with God. The kind that knows no understanding. Philippians 4:7 says, "And the peace of God, which surpasses all understanding, will guard your hearts and your minds in Christ Jesus." My peace came only through Christ.

How can peace come in such a crisis? I'm not saying things were perfect. I'm not suggesting I didn't have doubts. I only knew that I'd have peace and salvation either way.

I made a commitment that I'd live through this and get my life in order. I'd fight this thing if I had to. Fight for myself and my family. Three months of sobriety made this decision easier. I no longer had that uncertainty where a drink or drug gave me temporary or uncertain relief. The sobriety meant I had discipline and willpower. More importantly, I had faith in God and the trust that he'd give me the strength to fight this. To overcome. I finally began to understand that "I can do all things through him who strengthens me" (Philippians 4:13). That's my life verse. That's the one hidden deep in my heart. The one I turn to often in my Bible. The one that rolls off my tongue.

When the apostle Paul wrote that, I don't think he meant that he could cure any disease, or cancer, or someone else's cancer. I think he meant that he gave homage to the one that empowered him. We use the verse often in sports. I'm not saying a baseball player who writes PHIL 4:13 on his eye black and then hits a home run didn't use his own strength to do that. Rather, the athlete is telling the world that he only accomplished whatever he did because Christ gave him that strength. He or she placed credit where it truly belongs.

I had cried out and God heard my cries.

So, there began my commitment to God and my family that I'd depend on my Savior to provide the fighting spirit to overcome. Though I had said the "Jesus prayer" in the past, I'm not sure I ever really meant it. I now had that all-encompassing, overwhelming assurance that my commitment was true. I'd depend on him to guide all aspects of my life. That was the first time I ever truly felt saved. I knew I had a home in Heaven. That's true peace.

However, I worried how Kristyn would handle all this. She'd heard my empty promises in the past. If I told her I had made a new commitment to Christ, would she believe me? Could I really expect her to fight for me when I had failed to fight for us in the past? I thought about how divorce rates increase when a spouse has cancer due to the extreme stress it places on the relationship. She's the strongest woman I know, but had God equipped her to handle this? If she couldn't handle this, how could I?

Addiction and cancer are both terrible diseases, except the person has no control over cancer. Sure, sometimes humans do things to cause their cancer, but once it's there, there's little control. One can have all the willpower in the world, but that effect is limited. The sobriety let me see that more clearly. That is, I had willpower over some things but not others. The latter meant I had to have an enormous amount of trust in God. Had cancer come before my sobriety, I have no doubt I wouldn't have survived. I would have treated the symptoms by getting high and drunk. I wouldn't have trusted God for healing. I would have fought the cancer in my body by putting more bad things down my throat or up my nose. Cancer and the addiction would have raced to see which would kill me first.

I shared with Kristyn that I thought God was punishing me for all my wrongs. I told her how I had never had retrospection like this before. I had allowed drugs and alcohol to wreak havoc on my family in the past, but I wouldn't let cancer do that. I wasn't going down that dark road again. I asked her to join the fight.

"We are one. This is my fight too," she said.

The two weeks came and went until the day came for me to receive the results of the biopsy. I sat in the doctor's office waiting for them to call "Jason Hollen." I looked around the room as others poured over the latest magazine or scrolled on their phones. I wondered if they waited for joyous or awful news. I hated waiting as the office staff checked in patients and processed paperwork, going about their day without a care in the world. Of course, it's not their fault. What were they supposed to do? Assume I awaited the news of a lifetime and offer pitiful glances?

Kristyn sat next to me. Her father came as did her mother and grandmother. My parents didn't make it. I wore headphones and listened to one of my favorite bands, Godsmack. People assume their name is sacrilegious or that it's an affront to God. But it comes from a comical place. One of the members once had a cold sore, and another said it was a "godsmack," as if God had smacked them. Man, did I ever feel godsmacked.

After they called my name, I headed back to a treatment room to wait for the doctor. I sat there alone and surveyed everything in the room but didn't really comprehend any of it. It was all meaningless. Sitting there for several minutes seemed as long as the two weeks from just before surgery to this point. The room was quiet, but I heard faint voices in the hall. I waited for those footfalls as the doctor approached the treatment room and grabbed my chart. The calm before the storm.

The door rattled as he walked in, and we exchanged pleasantries. Before he revealed the results of the pathology lab, he wanted to remove my drain tube. That hurt like a son of a gun and briefly distracted me from the news. Then, I readied myself. My heart raced as he opened the chart.

The doctor confirmed that the tumor had indeed been cancerous, but also offered good news. It was only stage one, so I wouldn't have to undergo chemotherapy. They'd schedule reversal surgery to remove the colostomy. Although relieved, something I had learned in all my research caused me to question this.

"How can it be stage one if it caused a full blockage?" I asked.

He looked at the chart again and realized his mistake. It was stage three.

I wanted to scream, "Dude, this is life and death for me. Get it right!"

The surgeon had done the best he could, but I needed to call my insurance company and seek an oncologist. This wasn't the news I had hoped for, but at least I had the news. At least, now, I could fight this with more information.

My new doctor, an oncologist, told me that the surgeon had removed much of the tumor outside of the colon but likely hadn't gotten it all. It was stage three for sure. Another surgery to remove the rest wasn't an option, as there's only so much of one's body a doctor can search while looking for that needle in a haystack. The tiny cancerous cells can hide in every nook and crevice of a colon, and there's always the risk of surgery itself, the exposure to infection or the possibility of damaging other organs. I had asked my new friends in the online cancer support group for alternative treatments, but the consternation, the research, all the expert opinions led to one undeniable fact—chemotherapy provided my only option.

Before chemo, my oncologist ordered a second surgery to install a port catheter in my chest so they could administer the chemotherapy more easily. He planned twelve rounds of chemo. They'd pump my body with the cancer-killing drugs once every two weeks. They'd follow that with scans every three months for five years.

I had a huge fight before me.

I objected to the surgery, hating the thought of more hospital time, but the doctor convinced me that if the chemo drugs came into contact with my skin, I'd have wished I had the surgery. Complicating the matter was an abscessed tooth that required an immediate root canal. When it rains, it pours, right?

I won't pretend that I was a model patient. I wasn't necessarily a difficult one either. It's more that I simply didn't accept everything the clinicians gave me, whether it was a diagnosis or medication. Maybe it came across like I was a know-it-all, but it wasn't that. I realized they spent years of their life with education and long hours. Instead, I knew that not every medical professional knows my full medical history. Sometimes, professionals make mistakes, even if most work extremely hard to prevent that.

This second cancer-related surgery didn't start well. My doctor told me that general anesthesia wasn't necessary. This gave me such anxiety that I became argumentative with everyone at the hospital. The anesthesiologist came in and told me he was still talking to the doctor and not to worry. This calmed me down a bit as the time came to head for the operating room. However, I found out a nurse had forgotten my IV bag behind the bed because it had ripped out of my arm during transport. How could everyone at this hospital see what kind of shape I was in, and then make such a careless mistake?

Needless to say, this set me off with the medical staff.

Once they had the IV back in, I was laying on the operating table when the doctor came in.

"Do you know what you're doing? He's on the table backward," the doctor said to the nurse.

I was done. I tried to get up and escape, but this medical staff had great restraint skills and convinced me to continue with the procedure. The last thing I remember was the mask going over my face.

I woke up in the recovery area a few minutes after arriving. As the nurse began taking my vitals, I sat up and told her I was leaving. No arguments persuaded me, and I walked out of the hospital fifteen minutes later.

I could remember everything that had happened to me up to the point of falling asleep. The medical staff likely didn't understand that, as an addict, I had developed a high tolerance for drugs, and that included anesthetics. I'm not suggesting I know more than they do about drugs, but I know my tolerance levels for them. Having medication wrongly administered is a constant battle I face.

When my grandmother battled breast cancer, my father drove her to many chemo treatments. I hated seeing her that sick from the side effects, and now I worried how they'd affect me. Even after my surgery for the port, I looked at alternatives, such as RSO (Rick Simpson oil), that had been rumored to kill cancer cells. I had also heard of drugs that had yet to achieve FDA approval, but manufacturers only sold them in Mexico. I had exchanged money for non-labeled substances plenty of times, but in the case of these unproven cancer drugs, the risk outweighed the reward. No quick fix existed. In mid-May, six weeks after that Easter day, I started chemo.

That first day terrified me. Chemo "veterans" had listed so many different potential side effects that my mind ran wild with possibilities. I walked into the oncology center in Sugarland, Texas. It appeared like any other clinic. A cold, white hospital where no one actually wants to spend time. The place smelled of chemicals, and I couldn't shake the metallic taste in my mouth. A nurse sat me down in a recliner and hooked bags of fluid to me. The idea that this was like a combination between the electric chair and lethal injection crept in. How do you prepare for hours of drugs pumping into your body?

For two hours, I received a high dose of steroids to bulk up my immune system and hopefully prevent nausea and vomiting. Then came two to three more hours of cancer-killing drugs that doctors hoped would destroy any remnant of the tumor in or near my colon. Other patients came and went. I could tell that chemo veterans had their routines down from so many days in the chair, while us newbies received our baptism by chemo.

Most of the thirty or so other patients were women and lots of older folks. We all watched a lot of news and soap operas, but it being a hospital, I could hardly hear the TV over all the beeping machines. People across from me engaged in conversation, but I couldn't hear them. I wondered if they were complaining, talking about the weather, or gossiping.

I only experienced a slight burning in my body that first day. Not too bad. I survived it and returned two weeks later for round two, an easier trip, since I knew what to expect. I passed these hours in the chair reading, scrolling on my tablet, and listening to music. The IV hung from a pole on wheels, so I could take a walk or use the bathroom if needed. After the first few rounds, several hours every two weeks, I had my routine down. The doctor had prescribed oral steroids that I continued taking throughout the week. I hated every minute of it, but I endured.

Then, the side effects kicked in. The cancer drug caused neuropathy—damaging the nerves in my hands and feet. To this day, I cannot sit for too long; I have to walk to regain feeling in my feet. I now also have a heightened sensitivity to cold and heat, especially when it comes to food. Everything I consume needs warming or cooling. The drug altered all my senses. Rather than taste food, I could only smell it as it cooled and then eat it at room temperature. Hardly an enjoyable meal. This hot/cold thing may not sound like much, but you'd be surprised how much temperature affects the things we smell, taste, and touch. This continues to this day and may remain with me for the rest of my life.

The side effects are almost too numerous to list, but I'll list a few more to offer a glimpse into life under chemo. Night sweats prevented me from having a solid night's sleep and dehydrating me. I had extremely low platelets—the tiny blood cells that clot to stop bleeding—so cutting my finger posed a great risk to blood loss. I already had diabetes, but the chemo exacerbated that, and I was forced to correct that with medication. Fun stuff, huh?

Battling cancer is a lot like a battle with addiction. Every day you wake up and thank God for another day. In the cancer center, I often sat next to a gentleman named John. We developed a lasting friendship since we had hours together during our treatments. John battled stage four stomach cancer, which required chemo for life. We had many deep discussions about our faith, whether death frightened us, and what kept us going through this thing called cancer. We had each come to terms with our own mortality—a natural thought exercise when massive amounts of drugs are running through one's veins. Struggling through the pain of chemo is a day-by-day activity. I admired John's faith and thought it stronger than mine because he had endured this disease for so long.

One day we were having our blood drawn, and I said, "I'm ready to give up."

In response, he prayed with me and, at the end, quoted Philippians 4:13: "I can do all things through Christ who gives me strength."

I remember this moment as if it were yesterday. My son had quoted that verse to me a number of years ago and written it on notes of thankfulness that we proudly posted on our refrigerator. The verse had stuck with me. The verse kept coming to me in times of crisis. If a child could find comfort in this Philippians 4:13, and then an older gentleman found comfort in that same verse, and both quoted it to me when I wanted to give up—it had to be a sign. A sign for me to continue to fight for my life. If I could just turn over my fears to Christ, He would walk me through this. God's word constantly reminds us that He's much better at handling our burdens than we are. "Cast your burden on the Lord, and he will sustain you" (Psalm 55:22a).

I ended the chemo in September after ten sessions. The toll on my body made it so I couldn't endure another round. I had lost sixty pounds, was constantly nauseous, and took multiple medications to combat the side effects. The chemo pushed my body one way, and another drug pushed back. A vicious cycle. But, wait, there's more!

Life with a colostomy bag has its own set of ups and downs, except there are really no "ups." Without a normally functioning colon, the waste is redirected out through that ostomy hole in my stomach. Gross, I know. I have an attached bag that must be emptied before it's even half full. I always need to carry a change of clothes in case there's more than the bag can hold. I have zero control over this bodily function. None. I can't hold it. At all. It comes when it comes, smell and all. That includes gas. That's always nice in the middle of a board meeting when others hear it. All I can do is grin and shrug.

And don't you know I get plenty of stares from strangers. I certainly don't remove my shirt at the beach. God bless my wife, Kristyn, for changing that bag. My daughter will say "Mommy changes Daddy's poo-poo." Yes, God bless my wife. I hope this information serves as a public service announcement should you encounter someone with a colostomy bag.

One year after the cancer diagnosis, and a half million dollars paid by my health insurance company, my scans are clear. No cancer. Thank you, Lord! As I've said, many of the side effects linger. I have to monitor my temperature, blood pressure, and blood sugar, but I'm cancer free. Thank you, Jesus, I'm cancer free!

One part of this cancer episode and a side effect I haven't mentioned yet is the pain. Cancer hurts. The chemo hurts. It's all extremely painful. The oncologist wanted me to take an opioid. Imagine that? An opioid for an addict. Needless to say, alarm bells sounded off in my mind. I contacted my sponsor, and he shared the same concern. His answer shocked me.

"Have you thought of marijuana?"

***

From Kristyn:

That week of Easter, I could see Jason hurting, but I really thought it was just another Jason-pain thing. After everything we'd been through, I had developed an immunity to his issues. Don't get me wrong, I was thankful the "new" Jason hadn't abused drugs or drunk alcohol in over two months. I was on the fence, unsure whether he simply was having one of his moments, or whether this was serious.

We sat for dinner on Easter eve, a nice moment with my family where I didn't have to worry about him overdoing it with margaritas. He excused himself from the table, and I hoped he just needed some time to recover. I went to check on him and realized that he, indeed, had serious, unnatural pain.

"We need to go to the ER," I told them.

He declined, simply wanting to sleep. The next morning brought no relief, and he said he wanted to go to the ER. That's when I knew this was serious. I drove him but kept my Easter plans with family, thinking this would be a quick trip with a simple resolution. I later learned he had been Googling cancer for two weeks.

We arrived at a near-empty ER, so they took him to a treatment room moments after we walked in. They had him dressed in a hospital gown and nothing else in preparation for an enema. I stepped into the hall and saw him walking with the backside of the gown wide open. I thought, yep, that's my guy, and then apologized to the lady near me who had a shocked expression. The enema failed to alleviate the situation and an obstruction hindered the colonoscopy.

The radiologist came in and severely failed in bedside manner. When he updated us, he just blurted out, "You may have cancer."

What? Cancer? We both thought as we teared up.

The doctor realized his mistake, backpedaled his speech, and excused himself from the room. We sat in shock and looked at each other. After everything we'd been through, now this?

He came back in with a more subdued tone and told us that other things could be causing the pain. A surgeon booked an operating room, and the hospital staff showed the seriousness of the matter, treating us in an over-the-top fashion.

One nurse hugged me and said, "Honey, you can do this." I appreciated the small level of comfort it gave me. They took us to a beautiful, spacious room and kept killing us with kindness. I called all the family to update them about the surgery and the potential for cancer.

Jason's mom said, "You're not supposed to tell me that."

I knew what she meant. That this shouldn't (and couldn't) be happening. My dad and stepmom kept our two kids as I sat, waited, and pondered. All the past stuff we'd been through, all the heartache, all the fighting addiction didn't even enter my mind. Right after the surgery, the doctor told us that we'd now have to wait two weeks for the pathology report. Two excruciating weeks to find out if my husband had cancer.

I won't lie, when we received confirmation of the awful news, that we had a cancer fight on our hands, it angered me. I had already done the hard stuff, dealing with his addictions. Now this? Yet, Jason remained peaceful and calm. I had noticed how positive and upbeat about it he had seemed while video-conferencing with his sponsor. He had made his ultimate peace with God.

One evening, I sat on the back porch after Jason and the kids went to bed so they wouldn't see me cry. I called my dad.

"Why is this happening?" I asked him through tears. "Jason is doing so good."

He comforted me during that time. "We're all going to say our prayers. God has you guys."

Those weeks of waiting for the pathology results and then enduring a second surgery were the most difficult of my life. I bought two small pocket crosses that were carved from stone and made to be clutched in the hand. I kept one and gave one to Jason as he headed back for that pathology report. We had to depend on our faith more than anything else. My daughter was too young to understand what was happening, but we had to sit down with our son and explain cancer to him. The little trooper handled it well, asked his teacher for prayer, and wrote prayer cards with Bible verses for his dad.

Doctor involvement didn't keep me from researching every possible type of treatment. Though we wanted the most aggressive option, whether chemotherapy or something else, we looked into essential oils, acupuncture, and we even went vegan for a couple of weeks. Nonetheless, chemo remained the best option. On that first day of that scary treatment, I spent four hours crafting a Facebook post to share the news with extended family and friends who had not yet heard of Jason's cancer diagnosis. It was the hardest thing I ever wrote.

"Today is a day I never thought we would have to endure. As naive as it sounds, you just don't think it will ever happen to you. You hear the stories and pray for others, but never expect to be on the receiving side of such prayers. We live our carefree lives worrying about petty things, stressing about money, work, after-school activities, etc. Thirty-six days ago my view on life did a 180-degree turn. I was no longer asking God for more patience with my kids, or stopping silly arguments with my husband, or giving us more opportunities at work. Instead, I was on my knees in the hospital chapel apologizing for being so selfish and asking Him to save my husband's life. Today, my love, my high school sweetheart, my best friend, my thirty-three-year-old husband is starting one of the hardest battles he will hopefully ever have to fight. Today is day one of six months' worth of chemotherapy to fight his stage-three colon cancer. I have faith that God will heal him and is using this as an opportunity to show us what life is really supposed to be about. I sit on my back porch every night looking at the stars begging Him to place his healing hands over our family, to take this disease out of his body and give us the strength we need to fight this. I know God has planned this for us, and I tell myself that it must be because we are strong enough to handle it, and take this opportunity to help others. I share this not asking for sympathy or anything else other than prayers. Prayers for me, my two young kids, and my love! We are staying positive and know that this is the beginning of a new healthy long life together!" (Posted May 7, 2018).

So, there it is. Prayers and faith. But also colostomy bags. Don't get me started on how scared I was when Jason came out of the first surgery, and I thought they screwed up by leaving a hole in his stomach. I quickly learned the ins and outs, no pun intended, of dealing with and changing a colostomy bag. Fun times.

Chapter 10:
Funny Little Cigarettes

A well-intentioned church group produced the 1936 film *Reefer Madness* as a morality message to parents about the dangers of cannabis. The plea, "tell your children," would help them avoid marijuana pushers and the eventual madness caused by reefer. Clips of the film have lived on and been mocked in dozens of documentaries ever since. While most will mock the film's outlandish scenes, they'll still agree with the film's message.

Is marijuana different than hardcore illegal drugs? Is it really milder? Those are the questions I wrestled with while combating the side effects of colon cancer and chemotherapy. The pain was greater than anything I had ever experienced. Unfortunately, opioids are offered as the most common remedy for cancer-related pain. Millions of Americans take opioids with no complications, but the abuse of the drug has risen every year.

Let me issue a disclaimer. I'm not advocating for the legalization of recreational marijuana so high school kids can get high behind the school gym. I was specifically considering a drug prescribed by a doctor for medical use. I certainly don't want my son and daughter smoking pot. I'm aware that marijuana is a gateway drug that has led many on a slippery slope toward more hardcore drugs. I recognize my own use of the drug. You probably think I'm a hypocrite for even considering smoking pot after sharing all these horror stories about the illegal drugs I've consumed. However, even in my sobriety, there are drugs I must take. In fact, I've had great success avoiding abuse during my sobriety by following doctor's orders and using these drugs exactly as prescribed.

So, let me invite you to my line of thinking. Let me tell you why legally prescribed opioids frightened me to the point where I'd rather have taken my chances with marijuana. Like many of you, I had heard of drugs like hydrocodone or morphine but didn't understand their classification as opioids until recently. In essence, they affect the opioid receptors of the brain to relieve pain. So far, so good, right? Well, they also get you high. A lot of you might have been prescribed one of these after, let's say, surgery, taken a few for pain, and then correctly disposed of the remainder. Others enjoyed that pain relief so much, you finished the bottle even after your pain passed. A small, almost innocent overuse of the drug, right? Some, though, maybe some of you, wanted another taste of that high, so they sought a refill, telling their doctor that they still had pain. And thus, began their travel down that slippery slope.

According to the National Institute on Drug Abuse, opioid-related deaths have continued to rise at an alarming rate since 1999. In 2017, over 47,000 died from opioids, with nearly 1,500 of the deaths occurring in my home state of Texas. That's scary. No segment of our population seems immune from this class of drugs. It's not some illicit drug only sold in back alleys. People from all segments of society, from professionals to blue-collar workers, doctor-shop to find prescriptions of drugs like Oxycontin or Percocet. If that fails, they're calling a friend for a little help for the aches and pains, asking if they have a few in a near-empty bottle in their medicine cabinet. People have been known to acquire pain patches and suck on them for a quick fix. Caregivers and family members have been caught stealing pain medication from seniors for their own use or to sell. As with "big" drugs, such as cocaine, abusers are spending thousands of dollars, their use of the drug putting them in danger of losing their spouse, their job, and quite possibly, their life. This is the opioid addiction that, though not featured on the nightly news, has slowly crept up on society.

One of the worst offenders is synthetic fentanyl, which is trafficked from other countries. Local drug dealers use it to lace heroin and give it an extra kick. The user thinks they're getting pure heroin or an upgrade, but it can kill and has actually killed people. The more powerful carfentanil is used as a tranquilizer for large animals and is so strong that drug-sniffing dogs are sometimes killed by an overdose when they find it. Law enforcement wear HAZMAT suits when they encounter large quantities of the drug. Despite potentially being the most dangerous opioid making the rounds, it's often passed off as something milder for humans to consume.

Unlike sellers of street narcotics, drug manufacturers are spending millions in advertising to entice you to buy their product. I'm not suggesting they shouldn't develop appropriate drugs and advertise them, but with that comes a responsibility to help control their distribution and restore any havoc they've created. It's certainly not always the big bad manufacturer's fault or the fault of the doctor that prescribed the drug. But it's a huge problem, and those that contributed toward it can play a role in curbing the reckless use of opioids.

So, what does all that have to do with me smoking marijuana for pain relief?

At the beginning of my cancer diagnosis, the doctor prescribed me Vicodin and morphine, and it certainly helped. I had taken opioids in the past for pain relief, and surprisingly, never had much of a problem with them. That is, I never developed any addiction. Of course, those were my pre-sober days when I thought any drug could be a new high, and I had no respect for their power and influence in my life. Now that I was sober, and knowing their addictive nature, it scared me. In addition to the fear, I had developed an aversion to drugs. There I was, three months into sobriety, and looking at a long-term course of opioids—one of the most addictive classes of drugs in America.

I'd love to state that I simply endured the pain and avoided taking any of those drugs. But that would've been sort of like experiencing surgery without anesthesia. I don't mean I had acute pain like that from a cut; it was more like a bad flu virus where I felt miserable and my body ached. Simply rearranging my body in a chair or in bed caused hesitation because I knew the pain that was coming. If the TV was loud, it hurt. If everything was quiet, I had no distraction and focused on the discomfort. I contacted my sponsor to talk through my dilemma.

After a brief conversation, he brought up marijuana.

I certainly wasn't expecting that. He didn't say it flippantly, but he knew that marijuana had never been a problem for me. My past use had been casual or to help with the comedown after cocaine. I realize how that sounds, but it's not uncommon for drug addicts to mix substances to counter the effect, or to relieve the bad side, of another. If that sounds like a yo-yo, you're right on. I smoked marijuana to get high as a teenager, but that wasn't my goal now. I had quit alcohol and cocaine. I was done with getting high and, more importantly, had lost the desire to get high. My sponsor essentially suggested I choose the lesser of two evils.

In the past, putting a new drug in front of me was met whit little resistance. After my sobriety, I researched everything before putting it in my body. I wanted to know its origins, side effects, and interactions; the pros and cons from others that had used it, and anything else that might lead me to a more informed decision. I did that for marijuana as well, requiring a certain comfort level or standard with it before moving ahead.

One doesn't have to drive too far to see the letters "CBD" emblazoned across retail storefronts. What are these places? The CBD industry exploded with the growth of retail locations in 2019. The local hardware store or convenience store might have CBD products near the checkout counter. I'm sure many know CBD is related to marijuana but don't know the distinction. The CBD legally sold in store is certainly not THC, but they're closely related. Pot, hemp, hash, CBD, etc., all have one source—the cannabis plant.

Different species of cannabis—the plant—can be grown. Some produce low amounts of THC (tetrahydrocannabinol), the chemical that gets you high. If a product of the plant has less than 0.3% THC, it's considered to be free of properties that cause a psychoactive effect. CBD (cannabidiol) is typically grown without that high level of THC and won't get you high, but many believe it has other helpful properties, such as pain relief or anti-anxiety. Marijuana has more than 0.3% THC, meaning it can relieve pain but that it also has that psychoactive effect. They both stem from the cannabis plant just as lemon and orange are both citruses. Cannabis is a genus (family) with CBD products and marijuana two of its species. Similarly, citrus is a genus with lemon and orange two its species. It's not a perfect analogy and in some cases CBD can be derived from CBD.

My apologies for the science lesson, but the difference between THC and CBD helps explain why CBD is legal in almost all states. In addition, it helps to understand the nuances of different drugs, how they find acceptance, and why CBD is leading many toward legalization of marijuana.

That's the story on the recent CBD boom, but in general, cannabis has a long history in America. Its use goes back hundreds of years. One product of the plant is hemp, used for fiber and oils with medicinal properties. Again, hemp can be grown without a high level of THC. In the early 1900s, marijuana (with high THC) began making its way across southern borders and into the hands of those wanting to smoke it for a high. At this point, we return to *Reefer Madness*. The rise of pot use increased as America endured the tumultuous 1960s. Presidential administrations have declared a war on drugs, which has certainly included marijuana. The last fifty years have seen the largest efforts to introduce the smoking of medical marijuana as an accepted practice. Proponents boast strong evidence that its medicinal use rivals that of other drugs.

Studies have shown that it can help with pain relief, anxiety, appetite suppression, and other symptoms caused by chemotherapy. Some will point out that users have experienced short-term memory loss and that the smoke can be harmful to a person's lungs. Is it addictive? It can be just as so many other things can be addictive, such as cigarettes or energy drinks, but it has no chemical dependency. I won't let my son smoke pot, but I also won't let him smoke cigarettes or chug a beer. The pros of medicinal marijuana far outweighed the cons in my opinion.

So, I placed alcohol and certain drugs in one class. These were substances that I knew had been or could be a problem for me. I wasn't going there. Medications for my bipolar disorder, which are tightly controlled by my doctor and are not the type that I would ever want to overuse or get a high from, are in another class. The last class was reserved for marijuana, a short-term solution that I'd use, assuming it worked and didn't send me down that dangerous road. Deciding to try it was the easy part. Convincing Kristyn presented the hard part.

I imagined how the conversation might go. "Hey, Kristyn, I have this great idea, and my sponsor suggested it, and it won't be a big deal at all." That's the ridiculous way I imagined I'd break the news.

"What idea?" she'd ask.

"Instead of all these hardcore drugs the doctors want me to take for pain, you know...you've seen those opioid stories, I'm just gonna smoke pot. Cool?" Then I'd wince and wait for the inevitable.

Kristyn, hands on hips, "What? Are you kidding me? Are you crazy?"

At least, that's how I thought it might go. When I actually mentioned it to her it was worse. She was ticked! She couldn't understand why my sponsor would have placed that idea in my head. I told her his view came from a clinical standpoint. Once I laid out the research and showed her that the plan was methodical, not flippant, she understood. She had seen my pain and encouraged me to give it a try. She had actually done a ton of research during my initial cancer diagnosis just as I had and searched for every possible solution whether avoiding chemo or dealing with chemo and how each affected my pain levels.

The dirty little secret is that I had actually started using it the day before. I thought that if it didn't work, there wouldn't be any reason to upset her or cause worry. When I revealed that, she realized that not only had it helped with my pain but that my demeanor and personality hadn't been affected. I hadn't acted like old drunk Jason. No awful rants at strangers. She still had lots of questions. I confidently told her it gave me no craving for alcohol or cocaine. I had also struggled with appetite suppression, so I had hoped marijuana would help me with calorie intake since I had lost so much weight. It didn't help with that, but that would have only been a minor benefit.

I have to admit that when I first tried it, I didn't feel guilty; rather, I felt scared as if entering a danger zone. That first time, I only took three hits and decided to see how well that worked. I guess one could say I was experimenting with marijuana, but not in the usual sense of that phrase. I measured my use throughout this period. I certainly didn't get stoned and only felt a tad funny. An analogy might be that I got buzzed, not drunk. This was dipping my toes in water that, at the most, I'd only wade in up to my knees. I'd absolutely not get submerged. I treated it like medication, and thankfully, it worked really well. What a blessing! Yes, a blessing that I found something to ease my pain from cancer and the side effects of chemotherapy without trading relief for an addiction.

I didn't want to hide this from anyone. In addition to Kristyn and my sponsor, I wanted her father and my parents to know. I didn't want them to find out later and think my sobriety had been a lie. I wanted them to know that I'd never let anything master me again. I needed that accountability. This quote from the Apostle Paul states it well: "All things are lawful for me, but not all things are helpful. All things are lawful for me, but I will not be dominated by anything" (1 Corinthians 6:12). Just because I had made the careful decision to use marijuana didn't mean I had thrown my sobriety away. Everyone supported me on this other than my parents. I think they hated to see me going back to smoking something or going down a dangerous path.

There is one other side effect of my cancer treatments I haven't yet mentioned, a side effect that's not widely known. *Breaking Bad* fans might remember how the character Walt lost his hair and spent a lot of time hugging a toilet from the chemotherapy treatments. These are commonly known side effects. I didn't lose my hair, and God spared me from extreme nausea. As part of the chemo, doctors will order patients to take a lot of steroids, which have their own side effects. One of those is depersonalization—a bizarre feeling where a person feels as though they're watching their body in a movie. Imagine floating in the air and looking down on yourself. You don't have control over anything. I worried something would set me off into a rage beyond my control. You can imagine the anxiety one feels when this happens. Although seemingly harmless, it's scary. I hated it, and thankfully, the marijuana helped me through that.

Some reading this may ask, "If you had no cancer side effects, could you stop?"

The answer is simple. "Yes!" I've asked myself this same question many times and would actually go without it for ten to fourteen days to test myself. I passed each time. God gave me both freedom from the pain of cancer and kept me from addiction. My ultimate goal would be to never take any drug, even a Tylenol, for the rest of my life. I think all of us would gladly live free from ailments. I hope to reach that one day.

My aim with this chapter isn't to push for the idea of having a pot store on every corner or making the drug free and easy to obtain for fourteen-year-olds. The recreational use of marijuana, although not nearly as harmful as most other street drugs and certainly less of a problem than alcohol, is not what I'm pushing for in this book. But I am absolutely in favor of the medicinal use of marijuana, under a physician's care and when consumed in a safe place with no intention to drive or operate machinery. Use of marijuana should be safe, legal, and rare, if you will. Those are the same precautions advisable for many medications.

What does the Bible say about marijuana? It doesn't, but we can certainly be guided by the same verses that guide us on alcohol consumption. Ephesians 5:18 teaches that we should not "get drunk with wine, for that is debauchery." I agree and would tell anyone taking hydrocodone to be thankful for the pain relief but to not "get drunk" from it. It's obvious I'm advocating for the safe, medicinal use of marijuana. I believe with all my heart that God provided it for me when I needed it most despite my misuse of it in my younger years. Hopefully, my testimony and experience speak volumes toward this cause.

***

From Kristyn:

"Uh, I don't think so." That was my reaction to Jason's idea about smoking marijuana. In what universe could an addict think that drug was something they could consume without creating a new addiction? There had to be another way. Jason will need some drugs for his entire life to control bipolar disorder. I've seen him follow doctors' orders to the letter regarding those, so I'm comfortable with that. I had no comfort with any sort of recreational drug or alcohol. When we looked at all the options, there really only seemed to be two available. The kind that is highly addictive (opioids) and the one that he thought would not cause any addiction (marijuana). I ultimately agreed he should try it because I could see the pain he endured.

When you see a loved one hurting, desperation can set in. Anyone with children hurting wishes they could take the hurt for them, but it can happen with a spouse. It's a natural instinct. I wanted his pain to end. I wished I could take some from him. However, he had to get through the chemo. Unlike when I was the scared, young, new wife and mom, by this point, I knew all the signs of addiction. I looked for them, and thankfully, I didn't see them. Jason seemed like sober Jason, and that worked for me. He proved that he could use marijuana in moderation, only use it to deal with the side effects of chemo, and then stop for long periods.

What I appreciated the most was that Jason wanted to talk with me about it. He wanted us to make the decision together. We are truly two that are now one, as Jesus described for a husband and wife. He's allowed me to hold him accountable. His sponsor and fellow AA members do that as well, but he ultimately wants me to stay close enough that if there were even a hint of him falling off the wagon, I'd be there to smack him back on. I love him and our family too much to ever see him spiral down again.

Chapter 11:
Spiraling Ministries

I have a lot of ideas. Some move forward while others fizzle out. As an entrepreneur, I always want to explore them. A couple of weeks before my cancer diagnosis, I had one of those inspirations. I knew, not just thought, but absolutely knew that God delivered me from addiction. I don't brag or take credit in this willpower but state with certainty that God took away any desire to drink alcohol or use cocaine. Gone. Poof! That was no accident. I call it a miracle. I cannot dismiss that. God also gave me a burden to help others who are suffering the same affliction, as well as those that love these addicts.

For several days, the idea stewed in my head as the pain in my belly increased. Cancer derailed me, but only for a time.

With cancer in my review mirror, I put the inspiration back into motion. While visiting my friend Jeremiah at his home, I noticed the books he had written and how God had used him in ministry. That day, I knew I needed to put my story in print as a first step. I wanted an open and honest account of my story because sobriety requires honesty. An addict must be honest with themselves and others if they want to get better. My transparency might be more than most others would want for themselves, but that's the calling I've answered to birth this ministry. I didn't want to hold back or hide the ugly things because I want to help those who've done those same things. Take it from me, people can be much more forgiving than you might have ever imagined.

To realize this dream of a ministry, I created a foundation called Spiraling Ministries with a few others that share this same passion. Those reading this book closely will have noticed I used the term "spiraling down" many times. As in, my life was spiraling down. Out of control. Now I know there's a better direction. Upward! If someone can spiral down, they surely can spiral up, right?

Ultimately, my main message is one of hope. That no matter what someone suffers from, there are others who've traveled that difficult road, survivors who can confirm that hope and healing are possible. I agree that my story is unique, but there are survivors who can confirm that hope and healing are possible. I want to look anyone struggling in the eye and show them another path.

But why? some may ask. I'm a busy guy with a wife and children. I run my own business. What time or skill set do I have for this? Overcoming all these issues didn't happen overnight, and some issues I'll have to manage the rest of my life. However, I've tasted the victory of freedom from alcohol, and it's the sweetest thing ever. I've experienced victory over cocaine and other substances. And I'm cancer-free. Victory! I want to shout it from the rooftops. How could I not share this with others? We've all tasted something sweet and said, "You have to try this." Magnify that times a hundred, and that's how I feel.

If you haven't noticed, my passion runs deep on this. James 4:17 says, "So whoever knows the right thing to do and fails to do it, for him it is sin." That's how I feel. That if I simply go about my life and not help others, then I'd be in sin. God has commanded me to take this message to the masses, so others know they're not alone. A couple of verses earlier in the Book of James state that "You do not know what tomorrow will bring. What is your life? For you are a mist that appears for a little time and then vanishes" (James 4:14). I only have so much time on this planet, and I want to make every single day count for my family, for those that need my help, and for the Kingdom of God.

Like so many addicts, I assumed I'd always have those struggles. After all, the way I grew up and my challenges with bipolar disorder provided reasons for me to fall deep into pits of drug abuse and weekend-long drinking binges. I know all those paths addicts take to justify their actions. I know all the tricks of the trade, if you will. One might say I'm an expert in taking the wrong path. Since I know the way, I can recognize when someone is heading there or has already arrived. I can help them avoid that dark path or bring them back home. I'm no miracle worker, I'll leave that to God, but I do believe God wants to use me as an instrument for his work.

I've mentioned several people that tried to do this for me. No one more than Kristyn. I know I wouldn't be here to tell you this story without her. But there are also others, like her father, Randy, who has always had a forgiving heart and encouraged me to learn from my mistakes. I've had friends show up at hospitals and hotels to help when I've screwed up, yet again. And there was George, who I encountered in juvenile detention and took me under his wing to show how God's word could teach me, encourage me, and feed me. My sponsor, Harold, continues to speak wisdom into me weekly. My recovery dream team. One thing lacking from all of them was judgment. Not that they couldn't have or shouldn't have, but rather, they chose to love on me rather than simply judge and dismiss. That's the attitude I want to bring to Spiraling Ministries. We don't meet those we help with wagging fingers; we meet them with helping hands. We love them when they seem unlovable. We reach down for them when they're in that pit because we know there's a way out.

We can find a lot of Scripture that speaks to our reasons for wanting to help, but one little passage in the Old Testament is the main message I want all those seeking help to hear. "The steadfast love of the Lord never ceases; his mercies never come to an end; they are new every morning; great is your faithfulness. 'The Lord is my portion,' says my soul, 'therefore I will hope in him'" (Lamentations 3:22-24). There's so much peace in that. We are all sinners who continue to sin, but we know that a new mercy awaits us. We don't act in sin simply knowing He'll forgive us, but when we do stumble, He will show us mercy.

Someone reading this may want to tell me, "Wait, Jason, you don't get it. You think what you did was bad? Wait until you hear my story. I've done evil and vile things because of drugs. I've destroyed my family with my drinking."

I'm making three promises to that person right now. One, there's nothing they've done that will keep us from helping them. It might take different forms, but we offer a judgment-free zone to listen. Second, there's absolutely no evil or vile thing, no wrong, no sin, that God cannot forgive. Simply stated, you cannot out sin His forgiveness. Third, it's not easy. This can be hard work. It might be the hardest thing you've ever done in your life, but when you meet others on the victorious side, you'll soon realize it's worth the fight.

That's our vision and our mission. It's our "why." I say we because I'm joined by a team of people who are on the victorious side, as well as by those who've loved them and me through our struggles. They're a dedicated group that shares a passion for the hurting. When we came together, we found that several core values drive us.

We are a people of faith. That doesn't mean one must be a person of faith to seek our help or that one must make a profession of faith to overcome addiction. But we want to offer transparency that we serve a great God and ultimately recognize Him as the boss. For many of us, that redemption by God led to our sobriety. Everything we do is under His direction, and He ultimately gets all the credit. To Him, we engage in regular prayer for thankfulness, adoration, confession, and guidance.

We believe in the truth of the Holy Bible for all things in life and eternity. We know only one solution for the sin that separates us from eternal salvation. That Jesus Christ, the Son of God, came to earth as a man and died on the cross to pay for our sins past, present, and future. We testify that placing our faith in Jesus, and Jesus alone, is the only path to salvation. Once we receive that free gift of salvation, we know that God makes us into a new creation, that is, we're like a whole new person. Not physically, but we are changed inside and dedicated to His service. More detail and Scriptural support can be found in the appendix, but this describes our most fundamental core value—faith in Christ.

For two main reasons, we list honesty as a core value. First, we want to be honest about our stories. I've certainly presented everything that has happened to me and everything I've done to the point where you may have audibly said, "TMI." I chose to cover as many nuances to my addiction as possible to connect with as many people as possible. Kristyn's responses have been brutally honest to show what it's like on the other side of the story and to offer hope to those that love and care for addicts. Our ministry partners are encouraged to show that same honesty as much as they're willing so that all of us "not love in word or talk but in deed and in truth" (1 John 3:18b).

That leads to the second reason honesty is a core value and this one's directed toward those we serve. We'll never demand a full confession or for anyone to meet any sort of standard of accountability. We will, however, encourage those persons to be honest with themselves about their addiction. We'll suggest practical resources to help them in that regard. In essence, we encourage honesty, not demand it. We, of course, respect anyone desiring to keep part or all of their story private, so, as participants practice honesty, we pledge confidentiality.

Anyone reaching out to Spiraling Ministries will find compassion. To lead us in this, we don't know of any better example than Jesus. "And Jesus went throughout all the cities and villages, teaching in their synagogues and proclaiming the gospel of the kingdom and healing every disease and every affliction. When he saw the crowds, he had compassion for them, because they were harassed and helpless, like sheep without a shepherd. Then he said to his disciples, 'The harvest is plentiful, but the laborers are few'" (Matthew 9:35-37). That's how we see our mission. We want to act as a shepherd, for a time, to help those lost in their struggles. We don't suggest we have all the answers, but we seek to have a compassionate heart that can both meet addicts where they are and guide them toward a better path.

Family is central to our team concept. We don't imply that you must have a perfect family or that we do either. Rather, we know that true restoration involves a change in heart and physical well-being. But those changes almost always benefit the family. If addiction is one of the greatest enemies to a sound family, then restoration of one's mind and body can also restore damaged relationships. Much of the residual damage from addiction happens to a parent, spouse, or child. When I finally realized I was about to lose my family, I knew I had to change. They were and are the most precious things on earth to me. We also include friends and co-workers in this family core value. Healthy relationships provide one of the greatest benefits of victory over addiction.

Our final core value is the culmination and really the most logical step in the process. Restoration can have many meanings, but when we say it, we specifically mean a return to the body's healthy state of freedom from addiction. Imagine a recovering addict marking a milestone of one week, one month, or one year of sobriety. They begin to build one day upon another of healthy living with lessening thoughts or desire for drugs or alcohol. They live their life waking at a normal time after a good night's rest. They eat breakfast and kiss their family goodbye as they leave for a productive day of work. Their evenings involve enjoyable activities. This sounds like a rosy picture and, certainly, restoration doesn't promise perfect days, but it most certainly means much better days than ones that revolve around using and drinking. True restoration is the goal!

For us to accomplish all of this and truly impact lives, we intend to offer a suite of practical resources and connections. First and foremost, we're willing to be that first contact. On our website, you'll find a contact form under "I need help!" This might be for someone that is sick and tired of their addiction or a parent or spouse that doesn't know what to do next for their loved one that is addicted. We make no guarantee that we'll provide perfect answers or complete solutions, but as a first step, we're willing to listen. We promise to not share your information with anyone and won't contact you without your permission.

One of the strongest callings I have is to continue sharing the stories in this book with the audiences that need it most. I want to look at the teenager that is struggling with addiction and tell them it doesn't have to define their future. I hope to continue this work in treatment centers, psychiatric hospitals, juvenile detention centers and other places of confinement, where those listening may use my talk as inspiration for that day they return to normal life. I also want to meet young people before they begin spiraling, so I hope to reach schools and churches with my story too. I realize there are some dark elements in my life, so I'll always temper my talks to make them age-appropriate. I've already taken the podium numerous times at AA meetings and plan to continue to do that for my own recovery as well as to share my testimony with others so that it may help them. Any twelve-step program needs those willing to share their victories, both small and large.

We plan to continue the conversation through various forms of media, such as educational blog posts, social media that forms a community of survivors, a podcast. Our podcast will serve as a continual Q&A as well as a place to share both the struggles and testimonials of those walking the long road of recovery. A sample of guests will be spouses, friends, extended family, counselors, ministers, law enforcement, juvenile detention and treatment center workers, and of course, survivors. We'll invite the best of the best we can find in the medical field to bring listeners the latest teachings on addiction.

By some miracle, I have none of the lasting physical damage that can result from addictions. It's quite possible that my cocaine use damaged my digestive system and caused the colon cancer. I don't know that I'll ever know for sure. Regardless, it's important to educate those in addiction and in recovery on lingering ailments that drugs and alcohol may have caused. We'll always be careful to recommend the appropriate experts during any recovery process. We're not medical professionals and are not equipped to house anyone. Withdrawal effects can be immediate and can present a dangerous situation without the help of a medical professional. As one moves past that stage, regular visits and counsel from their doctor is an important part of the recovery process.

Someone reading this may think, That sounds great, but I don't have insurance. We realize that all of this costs money, and even that some insurance plans won't cover the treatment needed. Whenever possible, we'll try to connect those needing help to free resources from county, state, or non-profit entities, whether it's access to a medical facility or counseling services. In some cases, scholarships may be available for the neediest recipients. It's our hope and prayer that finances never prevent anyone from overcoming addiction.

As was discussed in an earlier chapter, twelve-step programs, such as Alcoholics Anonymous and Celebrate Recovery, are not only free, but they're some of the most convenient and successful forms of recovery. Spiraling Ministries loves the work they do and strongly encourages their presence in our society as well as their presence in nearly every nation in the world.

Although government can never be all things to all people, many elected officials are fighting for those struggling with addiction. The opioid crisis has consumed much of the attention in the media, but government resources can help with many forms of addiction. Texas Attorney General Ken Paxton launched www.doseofreality.texas.gov as an educational resource for Texans to learn about the harmful effects of prescription drugs, how to dispose of them, and where to find help. Another resource is the Substance Abuse and Mental Health Services Administration's National Hotline, which can be reached at 800-662-HELP (4357) if you need help or know of someone that does.

In one of my darkest periods, around 2013, I had been off my bipolar disorder medications. I loaded several guns in my car and took off. I didn't know where I was going but considered finding a spot and ending the pain from mania and addiction. I thought my family would be better off without me. Kristyn called Sonny, a policeman friend of ours. He contacted me and talked me out of it. He had a non-judgmental tone and simply comforted me. He was my suicide hotline that day. The National Suicide Hotline at 1-800-273-8255, or the Suicide Prevention Lifeline at 800-273-8255, can do the same for anyone you may know who needs it. While our ministry focuses on addiction, we know that many other afflictions can consume a person's life. We're certainly willing to help those that suffer from mental illness, experienced a troubled childhood, are dealing with that dreaded cancer diagnosis, or thinks of taking their life. They are all things I'm intimately familiar with, and regarding which God has called me to serve.

As a people of faith, we'll make our best pitch to connect you with other people of faith. I have no data to confirm this, but I'm willing to bet that there's at least one church in every town in the United States. I can confirm that some American towns have one in every neighborhood. In other words, there's one near you. Like government, the church cannot provide you with everything you need, but it can provide that community you desperately need as you progress toward a life free from addiction. Church is not a building. It's the people that provide fellowship, provision, kindness, understanding, and accountability.

Check out this definition for the church: "For as in one body we have many members, and the members do not all have the same function, so we, though many, are one body in Christ, and individually members one of another. Having gifts that differ according to the grace given to us, let us use them: if prophecy, in proportion to our faith; if service, in our serving; the one who teaches, in his teaching; the one who exhorts, in his exhortation; the one who contributes, in generosity; the one who leads, with zeal; the one who does acts of mercy, with cheerfulness" (Romans 12:4-8). So, the church is the body of Christ. That's a great family to have in your corner as you take the monumental step toward recovery.

In addition to resources on physical and mental well-being, Spiraling Ministries intends to provide resources for spiritual growth. That includes teaching lifelong disciplines, such as daily prayer, methods of worship, meditations on God's Word, and practical Bible studies. Some of those Bible studies are geared toward subjects related to the ministry: some examples are loving the addict for friends and family, taking our thoughts captive when we doubt or are scared, and not letting anything master us other than Christ. Some topics are more general, such as a focus on parenting for those of us who didn't grow up in faith-filled homes, a study on strength and courage, and one on perseverance.

I once heard someone ask, "What is your BHAG?" What a strange term, I thought. It stands for big, hairy, audacious goal. This chapter is about my BHAG. I hope and pray it exists to serve your BHAG. The question is not whether you can do this. I know you can. Many have. It's, will you do this? Is this the day you take that bold and courageous step to achieve victory? Philippians 3:14 appears on the walls of gyms and on the eye black of athletes. "I can do all things through him who strengthens me." God intends for that verse to apply in your life as much as in mine or anyone else's. You can absolutely do this.

Chapter 12:
Clean & Sober...and Thriving

During one of my therapy sessions, my counselor told me that I needed to have a mock funeral for my parents, not out of any desire for their demise, but so I could realize that I'd never have the parents I dreamed of and had to put that hope to bed. My parents are who they are, and I am who I am. Nothing good could come from me blaming them for things. This exercise helped me move on with my life without this feeling that something else needed correction. It gave me freedom to trust in my decision-making, despite whether they questioned anything I was doing. When fighting addiction, we many times hold on to some sort of crutch or reason we think the drug or alcohol is justified.

Kristyn remembers more about my past than I do from stories I've told her throughout the years. The more I progress in sobriety, the more I forget about that past. As spouses, we're truly one in the sense that if one of us is sad, hurt, attacked, or mourning, we both feel that way. So, she has difficulty with things my parents say as much as I do, but we're able to talk through it and move on. We really want our children to have a loving relationship with my parents and vice versa. Sometimes it seems like work, but it's worth the effort.

What a blessing that I'm free from those crutches. If they question a spending decision or something like that, I don't need to blow up at them or get drunk in response. I can simply understand that they have their opinion, and it no longer has to affect me. I choose to live by this principle. "If possible, so far as it depends on you, live peaceably with all" (Romans 12:18). That's my duty and calling as a believer in Jesus Christ. It's important I have this right because God has called me to share my life story with those who are caught up in addiction, battling depression, or struggling with mental illness. Many of them hearing me likely have their own crutch or some person in their life story that they feel "drove them to drink." I want to look them in the eye and confidently tell them I know exactly how they feel. I want to say that there is hope and healing beyond addiction.

I'm open to speaking to anyone willing to listen, but I'm especially drawn to young people that are locked up and facing an uncertain future. I do this with 2 Corinthians 5:11 in mind. "Therefore, knowing the fear of the Lord, we persuade others." I was that scared kid living in an institution, and although I had George guiding me in Bible study, I always had this underlying feeling that nothing would change. I'd get out, fight with my parents, use drugs, get drunk, and have another rage incident. I'd be right back in the same institution, in adult prison, or dead. That's how the addict thinks, as if they're stuck in a hamster's wheel.

The following statement is the most convincing argument I can make regarding the hell that is addiction. If I had the choice between enduring addiction or cancer, I'd choose cancer every time. I say that not because I'm currently cancer-free and supposedly beyond it, because I live in daily fear that cancer will come back. I think about it every single day. Cancer sucks. It's painful. It can obviously kill you. It was scary for my family. I hate that my wife and son had that worry.

The addiction is also gone. I'll never let it torment me again. I'll never let it consume my time, finances, work, or family. However, let's assume it did come back. It wouldn't require surgery or chemo. It would simply be there, antagonizing me. It might kill me, or it might not. It might take my job, or it might not. My wife might justifiably take my kids from me and kick me out of the house. I might get drunk and kill someone with my truck. That's addiction. Yeah, cancer sucks, but I'll take it over addiction any day.

One thing in my life that remains and might forever is my struggle with mental health, unless God works a miracle there. I'm thankful that it's controlled with medication and that my experience over the years has given me some advantages in how I deal with it. My bipolar disorder has neither evolved nor devolved. It's not changed toward the recklessness of compulsive buying or hypersexuality. It has remained mania that manifests itself in rage or the inability to stop a racing brain long enough to sleep.

The Apostle Paul has perplexed both theologians and laypersons with this passage of Scripture:

> So to keep me from becoming conceited because of the surpassing greatness of the revelations, a thorn was given me in the flesh, a messenger of Satan to harass me, to keep me from becoming conceited. Three times I pleaded with the Lord about this, that it should leave me. But he said to me, "My grace is sufficient for you, for my power is made perfect in weakness." Therefore I will boast all the more gladly of my weaknesses, so that the power of Christ may rest upon me. For the sake of Christ, then, I am content with weaknesses, insults, hardships, persecutions, and calamities. For when I am weak, then I am strong (2 Corinthians 12:7-10).

No one knows what he meant by this thorn. Since he references the flesh, one might assume he had a physical ailment or injury, but we don't know that. His point is clear that this thing that bothered him forced him to rely solely on God's grace and strength. While that's easy to grasp there are two other things we can try to glean from the ambiguity. One is that the "thorn" may not have been physical, but mental or emotional. Paul's writings on worry and anxiety could lead one to consider that as his thorn. It could have been fear or another emotion. The second is the ambiguity itself. Because we don't know what harassed him, then almost anyone can relate to this. Don't we all have some thorn that torments us?

Could my thorn be mania or something else; is it more than one thing? Sure, regardless, I know what makes me weak, and when it does, I can only find strength in Him. I'd love to tell you I follow these instructions to the letter, but sometimes that rage still gets the better of me. It's not so much the little things, but if someone were to ridicule my family or strongly criticize my work, it could set me off toward delivering a verbal barrage. My plan for this sequence of events is to pause, pray, and recite: "My grace is sufficient for you, for my power is made perfect in weakness."

God brought me a friend and spiritual mentor a few years ago that I previously mentioned, Jeremiah Johnston. The Lord gave him a tremendous gift for knowledge and application of the Scriptures. If you asked him a math problem, he'd likely return with a perfectly apt verse to solve the equation. He's passionate about answering those questions Christians often ask but which have difficult answers. His work as president of the Christian Thinkers Society takes him around the globe in a variety of venues. I state all this because he's a rare voice that has focused on how the church needs to broaden its teaching, care, support, and prayer for those struggling with mental illness.

By the "church," we don't mean only words from the pulpit but to the church's greater response in comparing the attitude toward mental illness to how the church responds to things like poverty, lust, or apathy. Many have become too quick to dismiss those suffering from mental illness as faking or using it as a crutch. While both of those things exist among some, it doesn't mean we ignore those truly afflicted with a disease. Some fake injuries or use a problem at work to garner sympathy, but we don't ignore all injuries or work problems. Mental illness might cause someone to sin, but we deal with that as we would any other sinner. We discover the root cause of sin and deal with it. We should consider mental illness to be like any other disease. We should acknowledge it exists, we should let those suffering or the loved ones of those suffering know we care, and we should offer real solutions.

For example, depression can have many causes, but mental illness is certainly a potential cause. It's easy to dismiss the depressed person and tell them to think happy thoughts. Everyone gets depressed, so we can sympathize with that. For most, it's a temporary emotion, like happiness or fear. I'm referring to chronic depression. The kind that can be crippling. Rather than dismiss the sufferer, we should let that person know we care, we take them seriously, and we (the church or ourselves) are committed to helping them. This is how serious depression can be for some: More people kill themselves than are killed by homicide. Suicide is the tenth leading cause of death in the United States among the entire population, according to the Centers for Disease Control, and the second leading cause of death for those aged ten to thirty-four. Did you catch that? The second leading cause of death for young people is suicide. A great number of these suicides find depression as the cause.

Linkin Park lead singer Chester Bennington spent his final days communicating with other musicians about future projects that included his participation. He sounded like a man with plans for the near future. He had been vocal about his struggles with depression and alcohol but certainly didn't seem like one that would take his own life. Two months prior, his friend and fellow musician Chris Cornell of Soundgarden committed suicide by hanging. He too suffered from depression. Bennington lost his battle with the disease and took his life as well.

What kind of church do we want to be? We want to be the kind that offers an open door to the Cornells and Benningtons of the world, to our next-door neighbor, to the student sitting alone in the lunchroom, and to that person we barely know walking past us on the way out of church.

I've tried to kill myself. Who does that? There can be many reasons, but I have a sickness in my mind that led me toward those terrible attempts. It's caused me to sin. It's done so many negative things. Imagine if the church proactively reached out to those suffering from depression. What if we preached compassion from the pulpit or established a ministry that welcomed those suffering with open arms? Some churches do this, but we need more. We need a change in attitude. Spiraling Ministries seeks to be one of those places where a person struggling with mental illness can reach out for help. We, of course, also encourage anyone in desperation to contact the Suicide Prevention Lifeline at 800-273-8255.

Although I've talked about mental illness throughout this book, I wanted to emphasize this element at the end to highlight what might be our most important work. While I'm absolutely passionate about helping those fighting addictions, I'd be remiss if I didn't make a plea for all of us to truly save lives by recognizing that mental illness is killing people every day through suicide.

There's a scary connection between bipolar disorder and addiction. Not all addicts have bipolar and not all with bipolar are addicts. However, you'll find reputable studies showing that sixty to seventy percent of those with bipolar disorder have some sort of addiction. I don't cite that to make an excuse for my addiction, but I believe that when we see one of these things (bipolar disorder or addiction), we should look for the other. I've included some helpful links in the appendix for all of the topics we've discussed in these chapters.

While a lot of books close with narrative summaries or conclusions, I think I'd rather answer your lingering questions or further clarify my positions in what has certainly been an unusual life story. Let's call it your interview of me. Stay tuned for the last question, which might be the most important of them all.

***

Do you think someone that commits suicide will go to Heaven?

Unfortunately, a lot of misconceptions surround this. Those of certain faiths would answer with a resounding "No!" They suggest that their tradition teaches that a person must repent of mortal sins (such as suicide) for them to be in a right place to enter Heaven. With all respect, I reject that, since there's no Biblical justification for that position. A person's justification for entering Heaven concerns their standing before God and whether they've placed their faith in Jesus Christ and Him alone for the forgiveness of their sins.

I suspect there are a couple of different reasons people ask this. Those that are considering suicide want to ensure their place in eternity. As with any sin, I'd encourage them to seek the Lord in prayer, asking for God to deliver them from that notion. We humans are masters at making excuses for our sin, yet, God has promised He always provides a way other than sin. "No temptation has overtaken you that is not common to man. God is faithful, and he will not let you be tempted beyond your ability, but with the temptation he will also provide the way of escape, that you may be able to endure it" (1 Corinthians 10:13). Others asking this are likely those who've lost a loved one to suicide and are worried about their eternal state. Comfort for them can be found in the following passage:

> Who shall separate us from the love of Christ? Shall tribulation, or distress, or persecution, or famine, or nakedness, or danger, or sword? As it is written,
>
> "For your sake we are being killed all the day long;
>
> we are regarded as sheep to be slaughtered."
>
> No, in all these things we are more than conquerors through him who loved us. For I am sure that neither death nor life, nor angels nor rulers, nor things present nor things to come, nor powers, nor height nor depth, nor anything else in all creation, will be able to separate us from the love of God in Christ Jesus our Lord (Romans 8:35-39).

How do I know if my loved one has undiagnosed bipolar disorder?

This is a tough question and one best handled by a medical professional. I can share some common symptoms, but they in no way mean bipolar disorder is the cause. It's likely you've spent time around or know someone that has bipolar disorder that is undiagnosed, or they've received a diagnosis but not revealed that to you. You may notice they become easily agitated, are jumpy, have racing thoughts, seem to have no need for sleep, and are overly talkative, and then all that is countered with indifference, depression, low self-worth, and fatigue. Of course, addiction is another symptom. All things can stand on their own, but they could be signs of some other mental health condition. Internet searches can produce helpful diagnoses but can also steer you in the wrong direction. I'd suggest you use that as a starting point, but know that numerous professionals are willing to help you.

The main character in the Showtime series *Homeland* has bipolar disorder. Claire Danes does a masterful job in this portrayal as the character works in a high-stress job and struggles to stay on her medications. Many of the storylines show her manic episodes and reckless behavior, yet she still gets the bad guy. Mental illness does not have to be disabling. We're fortunate to live in a day and age where medicine can make life normal for many of those with bipolar disorder.

Do you think smoking is okay?

No, I don't. I cannot really think of any redeeming value to smoking other than that some find it relaxing. That doesn't outweigh the harm it can cause to a person's lungs. I certainly wouldn't want my children to start this habit. For contrast, I know many can drink wine, enjoy the taste, gain some heart-healthy antioxidants, and never get drunk from it. One can make a valid argument that they're better off drinking wine for its good qualities versus the danger of drunkenness. I cannot drink wine. It's nowhere near worth the risk with my propensity for drunkenness to gain a few antioxidants.

"'All things are lawful,' but not all things are helpful. 'All things are lawful,' but not all things build up" (1 Corinthians 10:23). That's the verse that should guide us on things like this. We can think of all kinds of things that build us up but that others would find dangerous. Mountain climbing, serving as a missionary in a dangerous country, eating double cheeseburgers, to name a few. I can't make any argument that smoking cigarettes builds us up. I'm currently working with my doctor to quit.

Do you encourage recreational marijuana?

I'm probably not the best person to ask this. As an addict, I'm prone to abuse things like this. I don't place it in the same category as cigarettes but place it closer to wine with some positive attributes. But I realize marijuana can have some negative consequences as well. I wrote an entire chapter in favor of medical marijuana, but I leave the question of recreational use for others. We have some huge substance abuse problems in America. Meth and cocaine for sure. Alcohol. Opioids on the rise. Marijuana is pretty far down on the list. I'd caution anyone using a substance that may be somewhat harmless to *them* to realize their use of it, even in moderation, might lead to abuse by those watching them. Your kids are always watching. Your friends, family, and co-workers are watching as well.

Did you really quit cold turkey?

Yep! I'm excited to tell you I did. In reality, God did it. It's like winning the lottery. I wouldn't point to those instant millions and suggest I earned them. I'd say, I'm thankful, I will be a good steward with what God gave me, and I will invest it wisely. That's my sobriety. God gave it to me, and I'll now be a good steward with it. If you were to put a margarita in front of me or a line of coke, I'd have no desire for it. Let's hope the same thing happens with smoking cigarettes.

Have you fallen off the wagon?

I'm pleased to say that I have not. Not even close. As of this writing, I'm in my third year of sobriety. Aside from the cancer scare, it's been a wonderful two years of clarity. Of watching my son's basketball games. Of watching my daughter dance around the living room. Of looking at Kristyn knowing she doesn't have to constantly worry about me. Of spending Christmas with family and not wanting to sneak off to get high. Of focusing on my business and serving families after a disaster strikes. I'm solidly on the wagon, and it's been a blessing. "I will give thanks to the Lord with my whole heart; I will recount all of your wonderful deeds. I will be glad and exult in you; I will sing praise to your name, O Most High" (Psalm 9:1-2).

Are you angry with your parents?

I'm not angry. We visit them and they visit us. I love watching my children enjoy them and them enjoying my children. I want that relationship to flourish. I'd also like to improve my own relationship with my parents. We've both done a lot of damage to one another. I know, however, that I have Biblical direction to swallow my pride and work on this. "Put on then, as God's chosen ones, holy and beloved, compassionate hearts, kindness, humility, meekness, and patience, bearing with one another and, if one has a complaint against another, forgiving each other; as the Lord has forgiven you, so you also must forgive. And above all these put on love, which binds everything together in perfect harmony" (Colossians 3:12-14).

It's easier said than done, but if God can make me sober and heal my cancer, he can work in this area as well.

Do you fear your cancer returning?

As I mentioned earlier, it's a daily concern. As time goes by, I hope to go a day without thinking about it. Maybe that day turns into a few days or even a week. Cancer was so all-consuming physically, mentally, and emotionally that it's tough to simply forget about it. I have to make periodic appointments for a scan to make sure the cancer hasn't returned. Some call this "scanxiety" because there can be a bout of PTSD before, during, and after the procedure, while you stew over the results. However, I don't let it consume me. I continue to trust God with this aspect of my life. I spend much more time focused on my business, family, and this ministry.

Do you have friends and family that doubt your sobriety?

I sure do. I don't blame them. They knew all of my tricks of the trade to get high or drunk and sometimes joined me in that. Jesus had people from His hometown question Him and He described it this way: "'And are not all his sisters with us? Where then did this man get all these things?' And they took offense at him. But Jesus said to them, 'A prophet is not without honor except in his hometown and in his own household'" (Matthew 13:56-57). Now, I'm certainly not comparing myself to Jesus but echoing Jesus's sentiment that those that know you best are some of the hardest ones to convince that you've changed and are something other than what they've known you to be.

When we become believers, the Bible says we are a "new creation," but there are always skeptics. Any major life change needs proof to the outside world. All I can do is stay on the right path. It certainly took Kristyn awhile to believe it was real. For many, it may take them seeing three years of my sobriety. Or five. Or ten. Who knows, but I can only show them in word and in deed.

How do you deal with your past?

Saint Augustine of Hippo served as an early church theologian. Although it may be fiction, an anecdote about him is often shared. One day after becoming a Christian, he was walking down the street. A woman he had formerly slept with chased him down and said, "Augustine, it is I."

Augustine turned to her and said, "But, it is not I."

In that, he meant he wasn't that person anymore who was interested in promiscuity. I tried to quit many times, but I always knew I'd likely return to that high or hangover. Shortly after I quit cold turkey, I felt the magnitude of the difference. I'm not that person anymore. I'm by no means perfect, but I'm no longer a person daily focused on booze and drugs. This new person I am focuses on meditation, prayer, Scripture, worship, and utter dependence on God.

What is the most important thing you want to tell someone about the other side of victory?

A very real power lurks about seeking to destroy you. We call him the Enemy, or Satan, or the Devil. He has a certain level of power and demons under his control. But there is One whose power is not simply greater than the Enemy's, it's all-powerful. The Enemy controlled me for much of my life. He had victories over me. He stung me. But, check out this promise: "When the perishable puts on the imperishable, and the mortal puts on immortality, then shall come to pass the saying that is written: 'Death is swallowed up in victory.' 'O death, where is your victory? O death, where is your sting?' The sting of death is sin, and the power of sin is the law. But thanks be to God, who gives us the victory through our Lord Jesus Christ" (1 Corinthians 15:54-56).

That's the side of victory I now enjoy. I'm clean and sober…and thriving!

Appendix I

SPIRALING MINISTRIES
spiralingministries.org

VISION
To provide hope and healing to those facing battles and those who love them.

MISSION
To positively impact lives through compassion, practical resources, and sharing a message of faith and redemption.

CORE VALUES:
- Faith
- Honesty
- Compassion
- Family
- Restoration

Appendix II

SPIRALING MINISTRIES STATEMENT OF FAITH

Under God, and subject to Biblical authority, the leadership, managers/administrators, and directors of Hollen Foundation bear concerted witness to the following articles, to which they subscribe, which they hold to be essential to their life, and which are the foundation upon which the ministry is based.

I. God has revealed Himself to be the living God, perfect in love and righteous in all His ways, one, in essence, existing eternally in the three persons of the Trinity: Father, Son, and Holy Spirit.

    a. Deuteronomy 6:4

II. God, who discloses Himself to humankind through His creation, has savingly spoken in the words and events of redemptive history. This History is fulfilled in Jesus Christ, the incarnate Word, who is made to us by the Holy Spirit in sacred Scripture.

    a. John 1:12, 14:6; Ephesians 2:8-9; Genesis 1:26-27

III. Scripture is an essential part and trustworthy record of This divine self-disclosure. All the books of the Old and New Testaments, given by divine inspiration, are the written word of God, the only infallible rule of faith and practice. They are to be interpreted according to their context and purpose and in reverent obedience to the Lord who speaks through them in living power.

    a. II Timothy 3:16-17; Hebrews 4:12; II Peter 1:20-21

IV. God, by His word and for His glory, freely created the world out of nothing. He made man and woman in His own image, as the crown of creation, that they might have fellowship with Him. Tempted by Satan, they rebelled against God. Being estranged from their Maker, yet responsible to Him, they became subject to divine wrath, inwardly depraved and, apart from grace, incapable of returning to God.

    a. Romans 1:18-32; Romans 3:10-23

V. The only mediator between God and humankind is Christ Jesus our Lord, God's eternal Son, who, being conceived by the Holy Spirit and born of the Virgin Mary, fully shared and fulfilled our humanity in a life of perfect obedience. By His death in our stead, He revealed the divine love and upheld divine justice, removing our guilt and reconciling us to God. Having redeemed us from sin, the third day he rose bodily from the grave, victorious over death and the powers of darkness. He ascended into Heaven where, at God's right hand, he intercedes for His people and rules as Lord over all.

> a. Matthew 1:22-23; Isaiah 9:6; John 1:1-5; Hebrews 4:14-15

VI. Man was created good and upright, but by voluntary transgression, he fell; His only hope of redemption is in Jesus Christ, the Son of God. We believe that while we were yet sinners Christ died for us, took our place, and with His life's blood purchased the pardon for all who believe in Him.

> a. John 3:16; Titus 2:14; Romans 8:18; Gen. 1:26-31, 3:1-7; Romans 5:12-21

VII. We are saved by grace through faith in Jesus Christ; His death, burial, and resurrection. Salvation is a gift from God, not a result of our good works or of any human efforts.

> a. Ephesians 2:8-9; Galatians 2:16, 3:8; Titus 3:5; Romans 10:9-10; Acts 16:31; Hebrews 9:22

VIII. We believe that because God our Creator established marriage as a sacred institution between one natural man and one natural woman, the idea that marriage is a covenant between only one man and one woman has been the traditional definition of marriage for all of human history ("Traditional Definition of Marriage"). Because of the longstanding importance of the Traditional Definition of Marriage to humans and their relationships and communities, and, most importantly, the fact that God has ordained that marriage be between one man and one woman, as clearly conveyed in God's inerrant Scriptures, including for example in

> a. Matthew 19:4-6 wherein speaking about marriage Jesus referred to the fact that "he which made them at the beginning made them male and female," the Church hereby creates this policy, which shall be known as the "Marriage Policy."

IX. The Holy Spirit, through the proclamation of the gospel, renews our hearts persuading us to repent of our sins and confess Jesus as the Lord. By the same spirit, we are led to trust in divine mercy, whereby we are forgiven all our sins, justified by faith alone through the merit of Christ our savior, and granted the free gift of eternal life.

> a. Romans 6:23; Ephesians 2:8-9; John 1:12

X. God graciously adopts us into His family and enables us to call Him Father. As we are led by the Spirit, we grow in the knowledge of the Lord, freely keeping His commandments and endeavoring so to live in the world that all may see our good works and glorify our Father who is in Heaven.

    a. I John 2:25, 5:11-13

XI. God, by His Word and Spirit, created the one holy catholic and apostolic Church, calling sinners out of the whole human race into the fellowship of Christ's Body. By the same Word and Spirit, He guides and preserves for eternity that new, redeemed humanity, which, being formed in every culture, is spiritually one with the people of God in all ages.

    a. Acts 2:41-47; Hebrews 10:24-25

XII. The Church is summoned by Christ to offer acceptable worship to God and to serve Him by preaching the gospel and making disciples of all nations, by tending the flock through the ministry of the Word and sacraments and through daily pastoral care, by striving for social justice, and by relieving human distress and need.

    a. Matthews 16:15-19; Acts 2:41-42, 47; Ephesians 3:8-11; I Peter 5:14

XIII. God's redemptive purpose will be consummated by the return of Christ to raise the dead, to judge all people according to the deeds done in the body, and to establish His glorious kingdom. The wicked shall be separated from God's presence, but the righteous, in glorious bodies, shall live and reign with Him forever. Then shall the eager expectation of the creation be fulfilled and the whole earth shall proclaim the glory of God who makes all things new.

    a. Revelation 20:11-12; I Corinthians 9:24-25; II Corinthians 5:10

Appendix III

Suggested Resources

Suicide Prevention

- 800-273-8255
- suicidepreventionlifeline.org

Addiction/Counseling

- 1-800-662-HELP (4357)
- samhsa.gov
- psychologytoday.com

Bipolar Disorder or Other Mental Illnesses

- 1-877-726-4727
- mentalhealth.gov

Abuse

- 1-800-799-7233
- thehotline.org

Families of Those Locked Up

- prisonfellowship.org

Cancer

- 800-813-HOPE (4673)
- cancercare.org

I hope *Spiraling Upward* has blessed you. Would you mind posting a review and telling a friend about the book?

Join the mailing list at

spiralingministries.org

for news and current info about our ministry.

You will not be spammed!